Alaska

Safe in God's Arms

The true story of a young woman
surviving the wilds of Alaska
from man and beast alike
in the 1960's and 1970's

By
Joyce Tucker

ISBN 978-1-68197-769-0 (paperback)
ISBN 978-1-68197-770-6 (digital)

Christian Faith Publishing, Inc.
296 Chestnut Street
Meadville, PA 16335
www.christianfaithpublishing.com

Printed in the United States of America

Introduction

Alaska in the 1960's was truly the Last Frontier. It had recently achieved statehood as the 49th U.S. state on January 3, 1959, about two years before I arrived with my husband, an Alaskan Aleut. The population at the time was mostly native Alaskans of different tribes such as Eskimo, Aleut, Tlingit, Alaskan Athabaskans and others. In the village where I lived the natives were part Aleut, Russian, Irish and Swede. The village in 1960 was a small, close-knit community of about 60 people. They were all related to each other in some way. When I lived there I was the only white person from the lower 48th in the village.

I promised my sister, before she died of cancer, that I would write this book about my life and adventures in Alaska. I also wanted to write the book for those who may encounter dangers in life like I did. Many times I went to God in prayer and He was always there for me, and He will be there for you too. My intention for writing this book and sharing the personal and painful events I experienced is to give hope and inspire readers to always live their lives safe in God's arms.

Before Alaska

I grew up in Ferndale, Washington, in the countryside with three brothers and three sisters. They were all nice and I loved playing in the woods with them. I also loved riding the neighbor's horse every day that I could. We were poor but the house we rented was on a couple of acres and had an orchard with fruit trees. The owner had planted a raspberry and strawberry patch right by the house and let us pick and keep the berries from it. We always had a big garden, a couple of cows, chickens and pigs. We enjoyed going to church with my parents on Sundays.

I was 18 years old when I met Len at a roller skating rink in Ferndale. We started dating, going roller skating together and fell in love. He was 21 years old and a native Aleut and lived in a little fishing village on the Alaska Peninsula. Len had lived in San Diego for two years where he had served in the Navy from ages 18 to 21. He was just out of the service and was in Ferndale visiting a couple he had met while he was in the hospital as a teen. He had an accident in his village in Alaska when he was 16 and the doctors sent him down to Washington to have hip surgery.

Len stayed with this couple for two years while he was recovering. He went to church with them each Saturday and to a Christian School. When we were dating he would go to church with me on Sunday and on Wednesday and Friday night. I would go to church with him on Saturday. He didn't drink and I liked that as my family and I didn't either. He was always so nice and would bring me a box of candy.

He came to see me one day and asked me to marry him. He had bought an engagement ring for me. I was kind of surprised as we had only been dating a month.

I told him I loved him but I wanted to get to know him better before marrying him. He looked so hurt I really felt sorry for him. He said he couldn't stay in Ferndale any longer and had to leave and go back to his village and get ready for the salmon fishing season. It was now December and he said he would not be able to come back until next October and didn't want to wait that long to see me again. He wanted me to go with him now. I was afraid that I would never see him again so I told him I would marry him. My parents wanted us to date longer before we were married. I said I was 18 now and I was going to marry to him. They were nice to me about it but I could tell they were worried about me.

In one week my mother had made me a pretty white sheath wedding dress and my sister Dorothy made a beautiful wedding cake. We had a small wedding on December 22, 1960 at home. The minister, my family, a few of my friends and the couple Len knew were there. We stayed at Len's friend's house on our wedding night. We said goodbye to his friends and my family. I felt bad about us not being able to be with my parents for Christmas. I wish we could have waited and married after I had graduated from high school in June.

Alaska
1960 to 1975

These are entries from a diary I kept in a spiral-bound notebook. They are an account of my day-to-day life as a young married woman living in Alaska. I hope you see the hand of God working in my life, and the many times He was present, miraculously protecting me and delivering me from harm, both physically and spiritually.

1960
December 23

Len's friend drove us to Seattle where we caught a plane to Anchorage. It was my first time on a plane so I was kind of scared. I know he has to return home to go fishing, I just wish I had known him more than a month. I'm sure I love him and he loves me. I just have to trust him. I know he is a Christian man as he went to church with me several times and with the couple he stayed with while in Washington. I wonder what Alaska will be like, it's so exciting!

I wish I could have taken my wedding presents with me and the other things in my Hope Chest. We could only take one bag each because of the lack of storage space in the small plane we would be taking later in the trip. He will probably have everything we need anyway. He seems to have some money as he had a car and always brought me flowers and candy when he came to see me. I haven't asked him about where we will live. I'm sure he must have a cabin.

We flew over pretty snow-capped mountains, so close to them it was kind of scary. We landed in Anchorage about noon. His sister picked us up at the airport. She is very nice and is married and has two small children. They invited us to stay with them for Christmas. We had a nice visit with them. Because of our surprise visit, neither of us had presents to exchange. I felt bad about not having any presents for them.

After two days we returned to the airport for our flight to Len's village and were told the plane was having mechanical problems. We couldn't leave until the next day and we had to stay another night. The airline put us up in a really nice hotel and paid for everything. I love Len so much. I have never been intimate with a man before and I hope it will always be as wonderful as this. He is so romantic and bought me a box of candy. Tomorrow morning we will catch a smaller jet plane to King Salmon and then fly for three hours in a small Cessna plane to the village where he lives.

December 26

We left for King Salmon in the morning. The plane is so different than the jet we first boarded in Seattle. It is a lot smaller and has patches of material taped over places inside on the walls. The plane really looks in bad shape on the inside. There were not enough seats so we had to stand up in the aisle a few hours.

After landing in King Salmon, we caught a small Cessna plane to the village where Len lives. The flight was over flat land with no trees or mountains and lots of lakes. After a couple of hours we arrived at his village. It was a pleasant surprise to circle the little fishing village with a round bay that was ringed with snow-capped mountains. I could see a cannery, a dock, and very few houses. The village is about 500 miles southwest of Anchorage, the nearest big town. The nearest little village to ours was about 15 miles away. There is no place to land the plane except on the beach while the tide is low. It was really scary and I thought for sure we wouldn't stop in time before coming to the big high grass bank in front of us. It was such a short beach to land on but the pilot was very good and we landed okay.

We walked a short ways to a little tar paper shack close to the beach where his dad lived. His dad looked like he was about 50 years old and was very nice to me. The tar paper shack was only one room, about eight by ten feet, with two small cots, a wood stove, and a small table with two wood boxes for chairs. He said we could stay with him tonight. I can't wait until tomorrow to see the cabin where we are going to live. I wonder why we didn't stay there tonight, maybe it is too far away.

December 27

I woke up to the smell of coffee and breakfast being cooked. Refried beans and pickled salmon were different but good. I had to dress under the covers and there is no sink or running water so you have to wash up in a wash basin and use an outhouse to go to the bathroom. We went for a walk along the beach. It's pretty cold outside – about 45° but no snow. I asked him today where we were going to live. He said he would let me know later. I can't wait to see the house. I wouldn't want to spend another night in such close quarters with his dad again. It was really embarrassing.

Len told me his mother and father separated and she lived in Anchorage. He said that she was an alcoholic and was always in jail. He is one of seven children. He said he had two sisters living in Anchorage. The one I met was the oldest one. The younger sister is in a girl's reform school. He has two older brothers, Mark and Chris who live in Mark's house not too far from his dad's. Mark is the oldest brother, neither brother is married. He also has two younger brothers. Art is in the Navy and the other is in high school and living with a Christian family in Anchorage.

We went to Mark and Chris's house and I met them. He asked Chris if we could stay in his little house he wasn't living in. Chris said we could as he stayed with his brother Mark when he wasn't living in Sandpoint, another small fishing village.

The house was a tar paper shack with two small rooms, a kitchen and bedroom. The rooms were about 10 by 10 feet. No one had lived there for years. The house is not far from his dad's place and about 20 yards from the beach. We will be about two miles across the bay from the small store, cannery, and post office. I'm so disappointed and I can't believe I will be living in this tar paper shack. I had pictured a pretty mountain cabin like the ones in the movie "North to Alaska." The walls are big wood planks that don't come together and you can see daylight through them. The plywood floor is really dirty. The ceiling has wallpaper that is coming down and full of rat droppings. All the pots and pans are black from being used on a Coleman gas stove. There is a rusty wood stove that is broken and there is no bed or furniture, it is empty.

I have a lot of work to do. I felt like crying today because I was scrubbing on pots and pans for hours. Len was playing the guitar and singing to me. It's nice but I really wish he would have helped me so I could have finished sooner. I was so tired. This isn't the honeymoon I had imagined. Mark invited us to his house for dinner. We ate some moose meat which was really good. We slept on the floor in sleeping bags Mark gave to us. His dad let us use a pillow.

December 28

Len's dad had us over for breakfast this morning. Our house is so cold without heat. I'll be glad when the stove is fixed. I can't wait until everything is cleaned up. It is a sunny, nice day, but cold. We got some cardboard boxes from his uncle and nailed the cardboard on the walls after stuffing the cracks between the boards with the pages from a catalog.

We found paint and painted the cardboard a peach color and found some green paint for the plywood floor. He fixed the small cast iron wood stove so it would work and I scrubbed the rust off of it the best I could. I tore up the red and white gingham dress my mother had made me and the lace and taffeta underskirt that my sister had given me from Spain, when she was living there. I made curtains for both rooms. I tore up another dress to make covers for pillows. I probably won't have much use for dresses here anyway. His brother Chris had shot some geese and gave them to us. I used the feathers from the geese to stuff the pillows. I'm glad I brought needles and thread.

He found some boards and is making a frame for a bed today but I guess we won't have a mattress for about a month. Len's dad is ordering one from the catalog for us but it won't have springs. His brother gave us a table and Len found some boards to make a small dresser. His uncle gave us stain and varnish to paint the dresser. We used two empty big wood boxes for chairs and I painted them mint green with some of the old paint I found. We have to keep our food in a wood box on the indoor porch's wall because we don't have a refrigerator. There is no electricity here. Len fixed the wood stove today. I roasted the geese for dinner tonight, they were so good.

December 29

Today Len took me with him to meet some of his relatives in the village. He said there were about 60 natives living here in the winter. Almost everyone in this village of about ten families is related to Len. They are either his aunts or uncles or cousins. We walked along a rocky beach about two miles towards the village. We stopped at his very elderly aunt and uncle's house and visited awhile. The house was a tar paper shack and the doors on it look like ours and are so low you have to bend down to get inside. Some of the people here are really short, about four feet ten inches. They were very nice and offered us some smoked salmon and tea or coffee. The house was clean and neat.

We went to the village store by the cannery and I was really disappointed. The store only carries staples and a few cans of meat, tuna, corned beef and spam, canned fruit, canned milk and canned butter. Very few spices, salt, pepper, garlic powder, curry powder, chili powder, and Tabasco sauce. We bought some dried red kidney beans, flour, rice, coffee, lard and sugar. We packed groceries in a gunny sack made into a backpack, with a rope to go over our shoulders. I am going to miss the garden and orchard and berry fields at home.

He said he has no more money and the Alaska Packers cannery store will only give him $50 a month credit until fishing season in June. I am in doubt whether we can live on that amount until June. I didn't know he was so broke. That must be why he wanted to come back here right away. He should have told me. I could have worked in the cannery in Ferndale and made some money before we came here. There is no work here.

I am the only white person here. I have noticed that most of the houses are nice like at home except for no running water or electricity, so no bathrooms. Our house, his father's and one aunt and uncle are the only tar paper shacks in this village. There are no doctors, dentists, roads, cars, phones, TV's. Some natives have a shortwave radio. There is only one church, a

Russian Orthodox Church. Len said they keep locked up unless someone dies and a priest comes for the funeral or to baptize babies. A mail plane comes once a month if the weather permits.

It is really beautiful here with the snow-capped mountains and living so close to the Bay. The air smells so clean and the water tastes so good! I'll miss my friends and family and going to church, and my white cat. She followed me everywhere and slept on the end of my bed at night. I hope she is okay. Maybe I can find a kitten here.

December 30

I feel so happy, I really love him and the house is starting to take shape. The small sink doesn't work so his uncle gave us a pan to do dishes in. Maybe today we can find a hose for the sink to run dishwater onto the grass outside like the neighbor does. A long time ago there was a dock by the houses. There are a lot of big wood pilings from the old dock stacked up not too far from our house. The men cut up the pilings and use the wood for their wood stoves. There aren't any pine trees or other trees here to cut up for wood, just alder bushes on the hills. His uncle helped him saw some wood into blocks with a big long hand saw, one of them on each end. They split the blocks with an ax. Len chopped the wood while I stacked it on our small porch and he showed me how to chop wood and make kindling.

There are no magazines or books or newspapers to buy at the store. I will miss that as I love reading and always read magazines and kept up on world events. I'm glad I have my Bible to read.

His older brother Chris came and visited us. He laughs and jokes a lot. Len is more serious than his brothers. I think he is worried about being broke. Chris will be leaving this summer to work in Sandpoint. He fishes there in the summer.

Chris gave us a Coleman gas lamp today so we can have light tonight. He also gave us some Blazo (white gas) for our lamp. I found out tonight that a gas lamp's air only lasts about fifteen minutes then has to be pumped up again. It runs out of gas in about four hours and has to be refilled. The fumes from it smell awful and make the ceiling black with soot. The ceiling is only about seven feet high.

We use the outhouse in the day and catalog pages for toilet paper. For a toilet at night we use a big bucket with two pieces of wood on it to sit on. We don't want to go out at night because it is so cold. The only way to bathe is to heat water in a wash basin on the stove and take a sponge bath. Maybe we can get a big tub sometime to bathe in. It is so quiet here with no cars, planes and trains, just the sound of the ocean surf and the wind blowing. It is nice, very peaceful. I really like it. I love living in the wilderness.

His uncle is not married and lives in a big house about 60 yards from us. He keeps it very clean and neat. He made us a yoke out of wood to put over our shoulders to carry the water. The yoke has two small ropes, hanging down at each end and are tied to big bent spike nails that are like hooks. He made two short round dowels from a broom handle and nailed them inside the Blazo cans and made a notch in the middle of them for the hooked nails to go around. It is much easier to carry the water that way. The creek is about a half a mile away and up towards the hills. We went to get some water today, it tastes so good!

We went up to the creek until we came to a big waterfall. There was a small pond beneath the falls that was full of small minnows. We went home with the water and got a wire and bent it in a hoop shape and sewed it to the top of a gunny sack. Len's brother let us use his old hip boots and we went back up to the waterfall. The pond was surrounded by rock with just one opening. He put the gunny sack in the space between the rocks and I walked through the water scaring the school of fish. They swam into the gunny sack and we filled the sack half full and took them home. We gave some to his uncle and I fried some for us for dinner. They were so good. I cooked some beans for tomorrow.

December 31

I made refried beans for breakfast this morning. I washed some clothes by hand. I put up a clothesline over the stove to dry the clothes. He made me a rope clothesline outside and I cut some string to tie the clothes onto it. The wind blows so hard you can't use clothespins because they won't stay on. I had to untie the knots to take the clothes off the line. It was so cold my fingers would almost freeze doing it. I had to save the string for the next time, as there was no string for sale at the store. The neighbor lady gave me a washboard to wash jeans on, as my knuckles were bleeding from doing the laundry.

The beach is only twenty yards from our house. We packed some sand from the beach in a bucket and put sand under the house where the wind comes in. We found some old clear plastic to put over the windows to keep out the wind. He said the wind blows here all the time pretty hard, usually 40 to 50 miles per hour. It rains almost every day that it is not snowing. He checked the steel cables today that go over the roof and into concrete blocks buried in the ground to make sure that they were secure. Len said in the spring, summer and fall we would get twisters that come down over the mountains and make wind funnels, called williwaws. They are like small tornadoes but very strong. The wind would blow the house away if people didn't use the steel cables to hold them down.

1961
January 1

We heard someone shooting off guns last night to celebrate the New Year. I miss seeing fireworks, they don't have any here.

We had no snow in December but the weather has changed now. We have snow every day and it is a lot colder. We have to wear three layers of clothes to keep warm at night. We have a sleeping bag we lay on and one on top of us to keep warm. It's like camping out. The stove goes out at night and the water freezes in the water buckets.

Today we borrowed Mark's shotgun and he also gave us two pair of old hip boots to wear. We went hiking up in the hills to see if we could shoot some ptarmigan (grouse). It was really cold this high up in the hills and there was a lot of snow on the ground. The ptarmigans were hard to see because they were white against the white snow. He managed to shoot four, and we had them for dinner.

January 4

Len went out hunting with his brother Mark to try and find a moose today. They were gone all day but couldn't find one as it's hard to find moose in the winter.It is so good to have him home. It is pretty lonely without him here. Chris had been duck hunting and brought us some eider ducks. He said the salt water eider ducks taste the best of all the ducks. I'm so glad I know how to pluck the feathers off and clean them. My dad hunted ducks when I lived at home and I cleaned them. We used his brother's small propane torch to singe them. Len showed me how to cut them up in pieces and boil them in a pot and make a gravy paste and add tomato sauce. Then we put it all over rice. I guess rice is the main diet here. I hate rice. My mom made some rice pudding at home once and after I ate it I threw up. I'll have to get used to it. The ducks were really good! They tasted like pheasant.

January 5

Len and Mark went hunting for seal meat as we have no meat to eat. They came back with two seals. I helped them skin them with a hunting knife. I was surprised how thick the blubber was on them, about four inches thick. My hunting knife slipped and I cut my finger with the hunting knife really deep, and it bled a lot. Since there is no doctor in the village to stitch it, I just wrapped it with gauze and taped it up.

Mark invited us to dinner for some fried seal liver, it was really good! The other part of the seal meat is good, but you get hungry right away after eating it. We didn't hunt seal anymore after that. There aren't very many fur seals here. You hardly ever see one.

Mark comes to visit once in a while. He never stays too long as he and Len don't get along very well and always end up arguing.

January 25

The mail plane came in today. I got my first letter from my

family. I cried it was so good to get a letter from my mother. Mom wrote about everyone at home and it made me really miss them. I hope they will get my letter okay.

January 27

Len and Mark and I went out hunting ducks today. We went in the skiff quite a ways out from the village. We were going along the shore and saw a big sea lion. We needed the meat to eat so they shot it. They got up to it and had to grab a hold of it before it sunk. They tried to get it in the skiff but it was so heavy that every time they got it part way in the skiff the skiff would almost tip over. I think it was as big as the skiff. We had to let it go.

We looked up and saw a pod of Killer whales coming toward us. They probably wanted the sea lion so we headed for the shore. We stayed close to the shoreline all the way home. Killer whales are known for coming up under a skiff and tipping it over. I was so thankful we got home all right. We shot some ducks on the way home and had them for dinner tonight.

February 1

Len and I have been playing a lot of Rummy. He gets so mad if I win and throws the cards across the room. If I lose he calls me stupid. It seems he has a bad temper sometimes. It's not much fun to play cards with him. He can be so nice and kisses me a lot and pulls me onto his lap and is very loving. He is very romantic and likes to sing love songs to me on his guitar a few hours every day. He is a very good guitar player.

Today I cooked some spaghetti. I really don't know how to cook very well. I overcooked it and when he saw it in the pot he got mad and dumped it over on top of the stove. I think I had better learn how to cook right away.

I made some rice and mixed a can of tuna with it and it was good. The neighbors invited us over to play bingo. We played for pennies and had a good time. Len's cousin, Ashley, who is our closest neighbor, is sixteen and is married to a man who is Irish and Aleut. He is twenty years older than her. They are both really nice. She got married at twelve. She just had her fourth little baby girl with a lot of black hair, she is really cute. One girl has red hair, one has blonde hair, and two have dark hair. They have a big house with two bedrooms and a big kitchen. As she showed me around, I noticed they had a big feather mattress on the bed. I'm glad I met her, she is nice and the only woman within two miles to talk to. I'm glad she lives so close to me.

Today I made some corned beef soup. I cut up canned spam and canned corn beef. I put it in a pot with water, tomato sauce, a little bit of rice and pasta. I cut my finger on the can of corned beef while opening it. The tin was really sharp. It cut my finger so deep I could see the bone and couldn't lift the end of my finger. I wrapped it in gauze and taped it up. It really hurts. I hope it will get better soon.

April

Today is Easter. I miss going to church and celebrating Easter. I am happy I have my Bible to read. I used to hide eggs for my little brothers and sister in the grass. I wish they had some eggs here. I would hide them for the neighbor children. I heard the store might have some in the summer when the supply ship comes in.

May

The weather is a little warmer now about 50 degrees with the snow melting. It seems Len wants me to chop wood and pack the water from the creek more and more. I am beginning to think he doesn't like to work very much. He likes to play his guitar all day and play cards. I wonder why he has a nervous habit of looking in the mirror and combing his hair for an hour at a time. He has a lot of nice pretty black hair.

We walked to one of his relative's house today. I hadn't met them yet. They lived across the bay from us by the village. We had been visiting for a while and I was really thirsty. I asked them for a drink of water. They said it was out on the porch in a bucket. It was kind of dark but I saw a dipper on the shelf and a glass. I drank some of it and spit it out. It tasted like really bad rusty water. I saw another bucket. I must have drank from the wrong one. It was probably one catching rain from a leak in the roof or something. I will never forget that awful taste. I hope I don't get sick.

They have a small Pekingese dog, and when we left it bit me in the ankle. It had little teeth but it really hurt. I didn't say anything to them about it. I was afraid my husband would get mad at them. They didn't know the dog had bit me.

Today we woke up to rain and found out our tar paper roof leaks like a sieve. We have a real little attic that you have to bend over in. I climbed up into the attic by standing on the bed and pulling myself up into it and put some old cans I had found on the beach under the leaks. There were a lot of leaks in about ten places.

Every day that it rains I have to go up and dump the water from the cans into a bucket and dump it out. The first sunny day he will get some tar and patch the roof. We woke up to rain again today. Len's brother Mark let us use some old rain coats he had. The hip boots he gave us leaked so we had to patch them with rubber patches.

It has rained every day this month really hard. Nothing flooded because the land is slanted towards the Bay and the water runs into it. The creek flooded and the water was really muddy. To get the water clean we had to run the water through an empty sugar sack to strain out the mud. Then we boiled it and let the fine dirt settle to the bottom and strained it again before drinking it.

Len and Mark went out duck hunting today and got a few ducks. To my surprise when they got back they handed me a little golden baby fur seal. It was so cute. They said it was on the beach by itself with no other seals around. They thought maybe the mother had been killed by a killer whale. They were afraid a fox or bear might kill the baby seal so they brought it home. It was hungry and kept trying to suck on my black hip boots. I got a baby bottle from Ashley and put some canned milk in it. The seal wouldn't suck on it. I tried so hard to get it to drink. I put a hole in the end of a black rubber glove but it wouldn't suck on it. I tried just pouring the milk in its mouth but it just spit it out. After a few days we had to put it to sleep, it was starving. It was so sad. I heard later that they have to have their mother's rich milk to survive.

June 2

Mark came over and wanted to know if we would go with him to get some octopus to eat as the tide was low. He had made a hook at the end of a long, heavy, and thin round metal rod. We went with him and took a gas lamp and some gunny sacks. When we would come to a long flat rock he would poke the rod under it and hook an octopus and pull it out. They were pretty big and their tentacles were about three feet long. Len asked me if I would help and showed me how to take their head and turn it inside out and take the beak out of their head. Then I had to beat the legs against the rocks to make them tender. I tried but it wasn't easy. The legs kept sucking onto my arms and onto my boots and wiggling all over, even though it was dead. I had to pull the legs off of me and stuff the octopus in a gunny sack. It was kind of frightening. Sometimes they put Clorox in the water by the rock and an octopus would come right out.

We were able to find a couple of octopuses and take them home to cook in a big pot. It was so disgusting because the legs

kept trying to come out of the pot until it had boiled awhile. I took the purple skin with the suckers off and cut the white meat up. It was really good. I only cooked the octopus ten minutes. I was told they get tough like rubber if you cook them too long.

Len is so nice to me and is always kissing me and pulling me into his lap and so loving but he is very serious and never seems to laugh much. Maybe he's worried about food or money. We studied the Bible tonight and I told him how I had loved going to church on Sundays and missed going. He said the Church that he went to in Washington taught him that when you made love it was just to have kids. Married women weren't supposed to enjoy making love, only prostitutes. I don't think he is right. I never did read that in the Bible.

June 3

Chris came to visit and wanted to know if we wanted to go clam digging because the tide is really low now. We said yes.

We dug in the sand in one place not far from our house and in ten minutes had a gunny sack full of huge clams. We also dug by hand to get some big razor clams. It was really fun! I steamed a big pot full of clams tonight. Tomorrow I will fry some and make some gravy with curry and pour it over some rice. I'm getting used to rice now. I'm glad I knew how to clean clams and take out the poison needle. I had gone clam digging with my dad in Washington.

June 4

Today Len took my little hand-held radio apart and tried to hook it up to a copper wire going up the hill to get shortwave radio reception but had no luck, it was too small. I feel rather sad that the radio was wrecked as it was the only souvenir I had from my father. He had given it to me for my birthday. Chris heard we needed a radio and gave us a shortwave radio of his to use. This one could get reception. It will be so wonderful to listen to news and music again. You can also hear the Russians and the Eskimos talking on it. I wish I could understand them.

I cooked some red kidney beans tonight for dinner.

June 5

Today we put some tar on the roof so it doesn't leak anymore. I am so glad!

All the wildflowers and pink fireweed in the field by our house are in bloom and are so pretty. I have a wonderful view from my kitchen window of the bay and snow-capped mountains. It was sunny today although the mountain behind us makes a shadow over our house most of the year. You could still see the sun shining in other places across the bay, but it only gets sunny at our house from mid-June to October. It doesn't matter as the sun never comes out long anyway because it rains a lot, which I am used to from living in Washington.

We decided to take a hike up the mountain behind us as it was pretty warm today, about 60 degrees. We wore light jackets and took some bread and bottled orange juice (Tang). The mountain is really steep. The bottom of it is about 300 yards from our house. There are no trees on it just alder bushes. I really miss pine trees.

We hiked up the mountain about two hours. When we got to the top it was so cold the Tang was frozen and the wind started blowing so hard we could hardly stand up against it. It was freezing cold, and we were not dressed warm enough. The ground was flat dirt with ice on top. He went to start back down the mountain and I turned to go with him. I stepped on ground that had a lot of ice on it that went all the way to the cliff's edge. My shoes were smooth on the bottom and had no tread. The wind blew me towards the edge of the cliff. I started to scream really loud, I was so scared. I couldn't stop sliding. I could see over the edge and it was a long way to the bottom. He yelled for me to lie down and when I did I quit sliding about four feet from the edge. He came to me on his hands and knees and pulled me back to some bushes.

We were both starting to freeze by then and he told me to keep slapping my arms and to run to keep warm. We ran downhill through the bushes to get to the bottom. It was still warm outside when we got to the house. That was a really scary experience. I thanked God for letting us get home okay.

June 10

Today he told me he got a job on a fishing boat. It was with someone in a village about an hour from here. He will start fishing on the 15th of this month. He will have to help sew the seine (fishing net) and get the boat ready a couple of days before that. He would have to be gone a week at a time and would be staying on the boat. They fish for salmon and are purse seiners who work off of 25-foot boats. I was hoping he could have found a job with someone in our village. I am really going to miss him. It will be lonely here without him. I really don't want him to go.

June 12

We went to the store today to get a few groceries before he leaves. Len's brother Chris had to leave for Sandpoint to go fishing too. He is letting us use his skiff while he is gone. It has a 40 horsepower outboard motor on it. We had to get a 50 gallon drum of gas from the store. We have to put a hose in the drum and suck on it to get gas flowing into the gas tank. I tried to do it but got some in my mouth, how terrible that was! At least now I know how to fill the gas tank to run the skiff.

He showed me how to start the motor so I could use it in the summer to get groceries and gas and the mail.

Chris is also letting us use his shotgun and rifles, a .22 and a .30-06. He showed me how to use the guns and how to take them apart and oil them. He gave me some ammunition to practice on tin cans. There are a lot of Alaska brown bears around here in the summer. If a bear charges someone and they have to shoot it, they use a .30-06 rifle. He made a big bar with a two by four to put across the door on the inside so the bears can't break into the house.

June 13

I will have to try to find something to do while he is gone. I tried to start a fire in the stove for the first time by myself. I chopped the wood into kindling and put a little lard on a rag in the stove on the wood and lit a match to it. It helped to start the wood on fire. I made breakfast, walked with him to the beach and we kissed goodbye. I feel kind of scared staying by myself at night. He caught a ride with someone on a boat to the village where he'll be fishing.

I cleaned the house really good, and chopped some more kindling and wood. I went to the creek and got some water. It is only noon and already I have nothing to do for a whole week. I looked at the clothes in the Montgomery Ward catalog for about an hour. I am really homesick and miss my family a lot. I feel so awful I could cry. I read the Bible and went to bed early tonight.

I had some beans for supper.

June 14

This morning a cargo ship came into the bay and tied up at the cannery dock. Ashley said they come in to bring supplies for the cannery workers. They have a mess hall for cannery workers and a cook and a baker. They also put a few more things in the store like eggs, potatoes and bananas which are really expensive but bought up quickly. A banana sounds so good right now. Ashley loaned me a little money to get us some bananas. The tide was high and rose right up to the boat so I pushed it in the water and tried to start the motor but the starter broke. I had to take the motor cover off and wrap the rope around the fly wheel and pull hard on it to get it started. After about a half hour and almost giving up, it started. By the time I reached the cargo ship, almost everything was gone, but I did get a few bananas. It was so good to taste a banana again.

I made a pot of beans to eat and cooked some rice.

June 15

I was really lonesome today. I went to Ashley's house and visited with her. Her husband is out fishing too. She has never traveled out of the village and is very interested in the United States and what it is like. I showed her little girls a lot of new games to play. She told me some of the older people here in their forties and fifties have never finished school and cannot read or write. Most of them have never been out of the village.

Ashley loaned me her cookbook, and I am going to learn

how to make bread. My first try at making bread was a flop. It isn't raising right. I'll have to ask her what I did wrong.

I walked along the beach and tried to find some shells but found some big bear tracks instead and I came back home. I saw big bald eagles on the beach in front of the house. They don't seem to be very afraid of people. The natives said you have to be careful if you have cats because the eagles swoop down and take them away. They are the biggest eagles I have ever seen. There are quite a few of them here. I had some film left in my little camera and I took some close up pictures.

June 17

I woke up this morning and was already bored. I've got a bad habit of pacing back and forth. There's just not very much to do and I can't go hiking because of the bears. They are more aggressive this time of year. They are just waking up out of their hibernation. During hibernation they wake up every so often to lick their paws. Their paws are tender when they come out of their dens and walk around. They are also very hungry, and it makes them really mean.

I found some bright gold in some rocks today when I was walking on the rocks along the beach. I showed them to Ashley thinking I had found gold. She laughed and said it was Fool's Gold. I sure got fooled!

Ashley showed me how to crochet today. I am going to try to make a sweater. She gave me some yarn and crochet needles. She said all the women here can knit and crochet really well. They start learning when they are about six years old. The women knit the men sweaters with the figure of a deer on the back and make hats and gloves. They crochet pretty doilies. It will be nice to have a hobby to keep me busy.

I wrote some letters to my friends, family, and relatives today and will send them out tomorrow on the mail plane. I wish there were telephones here so I could talk to my family and friends back home. I miss visiting with people who I can talk to about world events. Ashley let her little girls come over today and we made some cookies. One of the girls stayed overnight with me to keep me company.

June 18

I went to bring my clothes in from the clothesline this morning. The wind was blowing so hard it had snapped the rope clothesline. The clothes were in the bay along the edge of the water and on the beach. I waded out and found most of them but I lost a couple things. I will have to wash them all over again. I set up some tin cans this afternoon and practiced shooting again and it was fun. I haven't seen any bears yet, just their tracks on the beach. I'll be glad when the tide is lower again so I can get some more clams.

June 19

I got up early today. It was nice out and I took my gun with me and walked along the beach to the end of the sand spit. It separates the bay from the ocean. There was an old wrecked 45 foot boat there lying on its side in the sand. I was able to walk inside and look around. Everything was rusted and falling apart.

I went back home and asked Ashley if she and her girls would like to go out in our row boat and try to catch some fish. She said she would like to do that. We had to pull the boat down the beach to the water. It was all the way up by the bank. We found some long round driftwood logs and put them in front of the boat and pulled the boat onto the logs and pushed it to the water.

We made some snacks to eat and took some string for fishing line and made hooks from a safety pin and baited it with bacon. There was an old dilapidated dock by our house with only some of the pilings left. We fished around by the posts and caught some flounder and small chicken halibut and English bullheads. It was a lot of fun. We took turns holding the little baby so Ashley could fish too. We fried the fish and they were really good, they tasted like sole.

June 21

I bought vegetable seeds at the store today and made a garden close to my house. It will be nice to have some vegetables and potatoes. We always had a big garden at home and I always liked to help keep it up. I hope everything grows good.

I miss my mom giving me a permanent and fixing my hair. She attended a hair salon school and liked fixing my hair. They have no beauty salon here. I think I'll just let it grow long and not cut it for a few years. Len's coming home tomorrow. It will be so good to see him again, I have missed him.

June 22

I got up early today and made a pumpkin pie and a chocolate pie. I made some bread. My bread turned out good for a change. Len came home about 3:00 today and we were so glad to see each other. He put his arms around me and kissed me and carried me into the house.

They really did good fishing, but they don't get paid until the end of July. I hope he will make enough money to buy some tennis shoes, jeans and sweat shirts from the catalog for us. My shoes have worn out and have holes in the toes. I wish he would let me work in the cannery. It will be hard to have enough money to eat on until then. At least we will have fish sometimes, and he eats while on the boat so that will help. He brought a salmon home with him and I fried it and it was so good! He likes the pies I made.

He has to go back in two days to help repair their fishing

seine, so they can go out fishing again Monday. Len played the guitar and sang to me. It was so good to have him home. He told me all about the fishing he had done.

We were lying in bed almost asleep when there was a loud noise like a cannon going off and the house shook so hard I thought it was going to fall apart. I guess these williwaws squalls (they are like small tornadoes) come down off the hills in the spring and hit the houses. I was so glad Len was home with me. I see why we need to have cables over our roofs with cement blocks at the ends buried in the ground to hold the houses down. This went on for about two hours with five of them hitting the house. Then it was over. The neighbor came running over to our house and told us the bow of our skiff was sticking through the wall of their house. The wind had picked the skiff up and broken the big rope it was anchored with and threw it about 20 yards into the side of their house. The bow was sticking through the inside of the children's bedroom. It had really scared them but thank God no one got hurt.

They left the skiff like that until morning as it too was dark out to fix everything.

June 23

We got up early. We had oatmeal for breakfast and I made some toast. We don't have a toaster so we have to put the bread on the oven racks to toast it. He went to the neighbor's house this morning and helped him fix the side of his house. They got our skiff back on the beach. He chopped enough wood to last me a week. The big blocks of wood are hard for me to split with an ax.

He took me to the village today to meet more of his relatives. I met his aunt and uncle who have thirteen children. They live in a big house with one bedroom downstairs and a big kitchen with a long table. Upstairs is an attic where some of the children sleep on three twin beds and some on the floor rolled up in a blanket. The mother is very organized and has all the children doing certain chores. She taught the girls to cook at an early age, and they do a lot of the cooking. Everything is very neat and clean.

She invited us to lunch and they served fish soup with the head and eyes floating in it. They offered me the fish eyes but I just couldn't make myself eat them. They were nice but kidded me about not eating the fish eyes. I also didn't like the dried fish, or the duck soup with the head and feet in it. The kids would sit on the floor or on wood boxes and eat bowls of plain rice and a little soup. The children are really shy and very well behaved.

The men played some poker with nickels after dinner. The women played bingo with the kids for pennies.

Some houses here are pretty nice, like the postmaster's house. It looked like the homes in Washington except for no electricity. Len told me the postmaster and his brother both lost a leg and now have a wooden leg. They were traveling on a boat with some women and children and the boat hit something and started sinking. They all made it to shore in a skiff. It was winter and very cold out and the men gave the women and children the blankets. Before help came the men were frost bit so bad they each later lost a leg. It was so brave of them, they were really heroes.

July 4

Len had to go fishing today even though it is the 4th of July. The fish are really coming into the bay now.

We woke up at 3:00 a.m. and I made him some hotcakes and homemade maple syrup for breakfast. He kissed me goodbye on the beach and the full moon and stars were so bright you didn't need a flashlight. I hated to see him go. I will miss him so much. It wouldn't be so bad if he was always here with me, but now he will be gone for another week. I went back to bed and slept until 9:00 a.m.

Guns were being fired in the village to celebrate the 4th of July as they don't sell fireworks here.

July 5

The vest I crocheted didn't turn out very well. It ended up way too big at the bottom. I wish I had a pattern book or directions to go by. I'll have to have Ashley show me how again.

Her girls came over today, and we made some peanut butter cookies. I had two pieces of fish left over, and I made some Russian fish pie which is a pie crust filled with cooked flaked salmon, onions, chopped up boiled eggs, and rice. It was pretty good and I gave some to Ashley. My bread is getting a little better each time I make it. I like to bake and make maple bars, donuts, and cinnamon rolls. It's nice to have eggs in the store now. We have no refrigerator so I have to keep them on the porch. I have to crack them open in a bowl first as sometimes they are really rotten. The older natives here make what you call stink eggs. They wrap eggs in leaves and bury them in the ground and them dig them up later and eat them. I don't think I will try that, I would probably get sick.

July 6

Today I took some string and a safety pin, put some bacon on it and tied it on an alder branch for a pole. I tried to catch a rainbow trout in the creek behind the house. I finally caught one and fried it. It was so good.

July 7

Ashley has a Malamute (part husky and part wolf) and a Cocker Spaniel. They barked a lot last night. There were huge bear tracks on the beach this morning. I carried a gun with me while walking to the store. I saw more bear tracks on the beach. It must smell the fish being canned at the cannery.

I also saw a small seal lying on the beach in the sun. He started making his way back to the water, it was fun to watch. I got close and tried to grab his back flipper and pull him up the beach a little bit to look at him some more but it was difficult. I didn't realize how quick he was or how mean. He tried to bite me and I realized how scared he must be and didn't bother him anymore.

I had run out of gas for the lamp at night. It comes in a five gallon square can and is very heavy but I managed to carry it home from the store on my shoulder while carrying the gun in my other hand. Len had to take the skiff to the other village to go fishing so I won't have a skiff this week.

July 11

I made some bread today and baked two pies for Len when he comes home tonight. I can hardly wait to see him again. I picked some wildflowers to put on the table and tried to fix my hair nice. Len came home about 4:00 and picked me up in his arms and swung me around and kissed me. He went back to the skiff and told me to stay where I was and close my eyes. It is my birthday today, and I wonder what he brought me. I was so surprised when he put a little puppy in my arms. It was so cute, a little female Cocker Spaniel that had beautiful long black curly hair and a white chest. He said he knew I was lonesome and hoped the puppy would help. I just love my little puppy. He had also brought a salmon home which I fried for supper.

We made the puppy a bed and played with her for a while. Len and the crew had caught a lot of fish and he was happy about that. He said he missed me a lot and wishes he was fishing on a boat from our village so he could be home more.

We will have to say goodbye again tomorrow morning. I will hate to see him go but I have the puppy so I won't be as lonely. I will be glad when fishing season is over.

July 14

I woke up this morning and the dog was crying and hungry. I brought her up on the bed with me to cuddle with. She is so cute! I opened a can of wieners for her. They don't have dog food here. I hope the puppy likes fish. I am teaching her to roll over and to sit up, she is learning fast. I took her for a walk along the beach and Ashley's girls saw us and came to play with the puppy. They really like her. The puppy likes to swim in the bay. I throw sticks in the water and she will dive in after them. She is so much fun, I love playing with her. I cleaned the house and read the Bible tonight.

My garden isn't doing well at all. The leaves on the lettuce have turned black. We are too close to the beach. The salt in the air and the soil is killing everything. I sent a soil sample in to the Department of Agriculture and told them what was happening. They asked how close I was to the beach. They said the soil was too salty. I guess I can't have a garden. We are only

20 yards from the beach.

July 18

Len was out fishing for a week and came home today at 4:00. He brought me wildflowers. It was so good to see him again. I think the dog remembered him because she was glad to see him. We had fish for dinner and he told me a lot about his fishing. It had been a cold and windy week and they didn't have a lot of luck catching fish.

Today we heard that Ashley's brother, who had been out fishing, had died. His fishing skiff was run by gas and they didn't know what happened but the skiff blew up and caught on fire. They found him and the crew but they all had died. I felt so sorry for them. Some of the fishermen now have skiffs run by diesel, which is safer.

July 23

We got up early and took the puppy with us in the skiff. We rode for about an hour to a bay that was quite a ways from the village. She loves riding in the boat. An oil company came to the village this summer and set up tents to explore for oil and gold or other valuable rocks. No one was around when we landed the skiff in a little cove. We saw where the men from the oil company had been mining. There were big tubs of different kinds of rocks. Some quartz have veins of real gold and silver, some had been split open. Some had purple or white crystals in them, and some looked like the lead of a pencil inside. We didn't take any of the rocks with us. We just looked at them and had a picnic lunch, and then left.

July 24

We went to the little store at our village. Two men from the oil company landed their helicopter on the end of the dock and got out. They tied it down because it was really windy. They went into the store and then they went back to the helicopter and got in it. We heard a big crash and an explosion and ran outside. There were big flames coming from the helicopter. The two men had gotten back inside the helicopter and when they took off they forgot to untie the ropes holding it down to the dock. The helicopter started going up but reached the end of the rope. The helicopter came back down hard, hit the dock, exploded and caught on fire. Because there were water hoses on the dock the men were able to put out the fire right away but both men had died. It was such a terrible thing to happen to those young men. I felt so sorry for them, and prayed for them. We didn't stay long as we had to go home right away.

We got back home just in time for Len to be picked up in a skiff by one of the crew members he was fishing with. I hated to tell him goodbye again.

July 29

Fishing will be over at the end of the month. I'm so glad but he still has to fall fish for a while, in September. His brother Mark is going to lease a boat and use it to fall fish. He said Len could fish with him and I could go along too. I would help cook and help stack corks and leads lines on the boat deck. We would be home every night. It sounds like fun.

Ashley came to visit me today and said her husband told her Len had been fooling around with a girl in the village where he fished this summer. It really hurt to hear her say that and it shocked me. I told her it was probably just gossip and I wasn't going to pay any attention to it. I know he loves me. I'll be glad when he is home. I'm not going to tell him what Ashley said about him.

Ashley and I were on the beach with the kids today and a mother bear and her cub came along the beach towards us. The bears were only about 50 feet from us and it really scared us. We grabbed the small children and yelled for the others to run to the house. A neighbor's Labrador kept between us and the bear and kept barking at her and running in at her and then running back again when the bear chased her. We stayed inside for the rest of the day, and she soon left the beach and went up in the hills.

September 4

Len came home today and doesn't have to go back to the

other village again. It was so good to see him again and he was so happy to see me and the puppy. We have to go Monday with his brother and start fishing again for two or three weeks. He made enough money to pay off our credit in the store and we will have enough to pay for about six months of food. We will have to get credit again for groceries from Alaska Packers. We have enough to get a pair of tennis shoes and jeans and some boots, and sweatshirts and warm jackets. Maybe we will make enough from fall fishing to buy a small oil stove for the bedroom. It gets so cold at night when the kitchen wood stove goes out.

Ashley and I told our husbands about the bear. They said they would have to shoot it because they don't usually hang around the houses like that. It was dangerous with the little kids playing on the beach. No one ever shoots the bears unless they really have to. The bear came back that afternoon along the beach toward the houses so the men went to the beach and shot her in the neck when she stood up on her hind legs.

They also had to shoot the cub. They said that if you don't shoot the cub it will never forget that you shot its mother. It will grow up wanting to kill every man it sees. I felt so sorry for them. I'll never watch again if they have to shoot something. I never would have, anyway, but I was afraid Len would get hurt.

September 5

Some of the older children had to leave today on the plane to go to school in Anchorage. There is no junior high school here. It is the first time they have been away from home. I feel sorry for them. You could tell they were scared, and some were crying and didn't want to be gone from home that long. Two women missionaries from Australia came in today on that plane. They will be staying in a small house in the village.

September 6

We had to get up early today and go with Len's brother Mark to the cannery and clean the boat he was leasing. We had to get it ready for fall fishing. I helped wash all the cupboards and stove and everything. It was a lot of work for all of us and took all day. We came home for lunch but then went right back to work. They had to patch the holes in the net and Len showed me how to sew seine. It reminds me of crocheting. They bought enough groceries to put on the boat to last a week. He showed me how to work on the deck of the boat and how to operate the power block and stack the net leads on one side of the boat and the corks on the other. I will be cooking too. We are all ready to go.

I was really tired when I got home tonight. When Len is home he needs the lamp to read by so I have to use the flashlight to cook by as we only have one gas lamp.

Ashley said she would feed our dog during the day. I made the dog some oatmeal, hotcakes, and left a can of wieners for him to eat.

September 7

They told me how dangerous fishing can be and to be careful. You can't have any rings on your fingers. One young man from the states was fishing with a ring on and it got tangled in the net as it was going out and pulled him off the boat and overboard. He was very fortunate not to have drowned. Another time a young man was working on a fishing boat and was down in the haul of the boat. The boat motor was running and he touched the shaft that was spinning around and cut off his finger.

It was my first day out to sea on the boat, and while inside the cabin cooking I got seasick. It was such bad weather and so rough that I had trouble standing up to cook. I did manage to finish cooking a spaghetti dinner. Then I went upstairs and threw up over the side of the boat. They told me to stay up on deck by the cabin. I was amazed when I saw how big and deep the waves were. There was another boat following behind us and when it went over a big wave you could see the bottom of the boat all the way back to the stern, and it would slap back down with a bang. We were staying close to the shoreline.

We pulled into a little bay and anchored and stayed for the night. We had to use a small bucket for a toilet. The beds were pretty hard but okay. There was no wind in this cove so I wasn't seasick anymore.

About three o'clock in the morning his brother woke us up. I sat up and hit my head on the bunk above me. He wanted us to come and look outside. The moon was full and it was as bright as day. Fish were jumping out of the water all around us and shimmered in the moonlight. The fish jumping out of the water meant there was a big school of fish. Mark thought it was light enough out with the moon being so bright that we could make a haul and catch the fish. Len jumped in the skiff and we pulled up the anchor. We caught a lot of fish and filled the boat with them.

The next morning we left the cove and checked on the weather. According to the shortwave radio, the wind had gone down. We had a nice trip back to the village, and they let me steer the boat some. It was really fun! The sun was out and the water was pretty calm. Len and I sat up by the bow of the boat in the sun, it was really nice. We delivered the fish to the cannery and they let me dock the boat. It was very difficult but they helped guide me. We had to stand in the hull of the boat and throw all the fish by hand into a big net that was lowered from the dock. Mark wanted to go out again while the fish were running so we went home and picked up our dog and took him with us out fishing. The dog really enjoys being on the boat. It was a beautiful day and we saw a couple of whales spouting nearby. The fishing was good again today.

When we got home today we heard that Len's dad had died of a heart attack while we were fishing. I felt so sorry for Len. His dad was only 50. Len's brother Chris flew in from Sandpoint for the funeral. Their brother Art came in also, he is in the Navy. He was able to get a leave of absence because of his father's death. Their two sisters were not able to come.

The family had a small memorial service at the Russian Orthodox Church on the hill overlooking the village and buried him on the hill in back of the church. A priest had come to the village and said some things in Latin and passed candles around and we all lit them. The relatives went to Len's uncle's house by the church where they had a homemade keg of beer. We didn't stay because Len didn't like the idea of everyone having a party and drinking when his dad had just died. We rode home in the boat with Mark, Chris, and Art.

Len talked about his dad some before we went to sleep. I guess they hadn't been very close. When he was young his dad used a whip on him if he did something wrong. His dad was so mean to his mom that she left him and went to Anchorage.

September 9

We woke up to rain and a windy day. Len and Mark didn't feel like going fishing today. They all went to their dad's house and looked through some of his things and divided them. There were very few personal things and nothing of value. Chris will stay in his dad's house for a few days. When he leaves he will give us the blankets, sheets and pillows. He will fish with Len and Mark for the rest of the fall season and I'll stay home.

Mark, Chris, and Art came over and visited with Len for a while and then went home. Art is really nice. He was still in his Navy uniform. He seems so young to be in the service. He's really shy and doesn't say much. His brothers have fun teasing him.

Art will stay with Mark while he's here. He's going fishing with them this week and staying with Mark tonight. I made salmon for dinner and some pies and Art ate at our house.

Len and I put on some rain coats and went for a hike in the rain.

September 11

The sun is out today. Len and his brothers left early this morning to go fishing. They will stay out for a week to go farther along the coast. I'll miss Len again, and I am glad for the puppy. She is getting bigger now and has learned her tricks very well. She can roll over and sit up now.

I went with Ashley and we walked about a mile to the sand spit and picked some blue currants and salmon berries. They are really good and the children helped, so we got a few buckets of berries. I'm glad I brought the rifle with us. On the way back home we heard a loud noise from the bank above the beach and two bears went running up the hill. It is amazing how fast they can run. When we got back to the house Ashley showed me how to take the little blue currant berries and mix them with a little bit of Crisco and sugar. They were very good that way.

I decided to try and get a fish from the creek today. Len had made a spear for me and I went to the creek behind the house and after several tries managed to spear a salmon. I boiled it for dinner and had rice and the berries with it. I think they will be back from fishing tomorrow. There is a storm coming this way.

Len and his brothers got home this afternoon. They were pretty tired and said they caught some fish but not a lot. Tomorrow they will sew the seine and clean up the boat and I'll go help them. They enjoyed some donuts and maple bars I had made. Tomorrow they are going to try to get some ducks.

September 12

They all went out duck hunting on the bay with two skiffs. They came back two hours later with about thirty saltwater ducks. They took some ducks to their relatives in the village. I plucked four ducks and made a big pot of duck stew to pour over rice. The ducks were a nice change from fish. Len played the guitar and sang to me while I cooked.

We all went to the boat at the dock and cleaned it up and put everything away for the year. They pull the boat up on the shore onto a dry dock for the winter.

September 14

Today the weather is beautiful and Art wants to go moose hunting with Len, Chris, Mark and me before he has to go back to the Navy. We are all going in two skiffs. It is about an hour ride to a trap shack Len's uncle owns on a beach called Ocean Beach. We will try to get a moose in one day so we don't have to stay overnight.

We landed the skiffs very carefully on Ocean Beach because of the huge waves. We had to run the skiff full speed, about 30 mph, up on the beach and lift up the motor at the right time so the skiff will slide up the beach. Then we had to hurry and jump out and turn the skiff around so the bow is facing the next incoming wave and drag it farther up the beach so it wouldn't get full of water. We found some round driftwood logs to put under the skiffs and pulled them up above the tide line. We saw bear tracks right away. They were really big and fresh. When we got to the trap shack we saw a bull moose and a female, and a baby moose up on the hill.

I stayed at the trap shack when they left to go hunt the moose. The trap shack was built into the side of a dirt cliff and its tar paper roof is even with the cliff. The front of the shack is tar paper and inside it has rough wood floors and a wood stove and two small rooms. There were two cots for beds and a kitchen with a small wood table and wood boxes for chairs.

Everything was very clean and neat except for the mice. I could see them running around every once and awhile. In the bottom cupboards there were hundreds of daddy long leg spiders stacked on top of each other, from the top to the bottom of the cupboard. It was so horrible I quickly closed the cupboard door. I found a creek outside and boiled some water to wash cups and started a fire with some driftwood, and made coffee for them. I looked around and found some real old comic books and old books. There was also a full size poster of Marilyn Monroe on one of the doors.

They came back two hours later. They said the moose went into the creek and Art jumped on its back and they took a picture of it. He got off and they shot the moose and brought back what they could. They wanted to go back and get what was left and said they would be back in about an hour.

When they got back from hunting the tide had come in and made it easier to push the skiffs into the water and load the meat in. The moose meat made the skiff ride very low in the water. We had to be very careful not to capsize with the big waves coming in. I had to stand in the bow with an oar in the water to keep the bow headed into the waves so the skiff wouldn't flip over. I was afraid I would not be strong enough to do it but I did. We made it home okay but it was a long, slow ride. They hung the meat up until we could cut it up. The puppy was really glad to see us. I was so tired that I just heated up beans for supper tonight.

September 15

Art has to go back to the Navy today. He will be missed a lot by his brothers. We took him to the airplane and said goodbye to him. We went to the cannery and asked the office superintendent if we could use their big freezer to store some of the moose meat and fish for the winter. Other people in the village had also asked the superintendent so he agreed to let us. It is the only place in the village with electricity. Everyone will put their names on their boxes of meat.

September 16

Today we cut up the moose. The men sawed the big bones into small pieces and cut the rib rack and I cut and packed all the smaller pieces into steaks and stew meat. I borrowed a neighbor's meat grinder and made moose burgers. We divided the moose meat in half with Mark. Chris will be leaving to go work in Sandpoint soon. We put all the meat in boxes and took it to the freezer except some that will last a few days without refrigeration.

I made some moose steaks and gravy for supper. It tasted just like beef and really tender. Because of the vegetation the moose eat here their meat doesn't have a strong wild taste.

September 17

Mark and Len's uncle came by today and wanted us to go with him to get fish from the river where they go to spawn. We will freeze and smoke some. We left with a small gill net and three skiffs and it took an hour to get to the river. We stopped at a small village with a small dock and store and we bought more gas.

As we drove along the river you could see families of bears eating fish. Bald eagles were also along the beach eating the fish that had come to spawn. We came to a lake and went ashore. We saw small bear tracks leading to a dead bear someone had shot. I felt sorry for him. I was surprised a big 10-foot bear had such small feet. I learned you can't always tell how big a bear is by the size of its tracks. The bears eat only the bellies and heads of fish. The seagulls like the eyes the best. There were dead fish all over the banks of the lake. I was surprised at how much the fish varied in looks when they went up river to spawn. The pink salmon or humpback salmon now had a big hump on their back and the dog salmon had big hooked noses and their color was dark maroon.

We saw a school of fish jumping in the lake and made a circle around them with the gill net and pulled it ashore. We handpicked all the fish out of the gill net and put them in the skiffs. We had about 150 fish in each skiff. We started back and had to go very slow. With so much weight our skiffs were really low in the water. We got to the middle of the lake and the wind came up fast. The water started to form into big deep waves which were coming into the skiff. I used a five gallon bucket and started bailing fast to keep up with the water coming in. I was scared we were going to sink.

Mark yelled for us to head for shore. We made it to the side of the lake where the wind wasn't so bad. Lakes can be dangerous. In fresh water, boats are less buoyant than in the bay's salt water. We stayed along the shoreline but by doing this we wouldn't get home before dark. Because there was enough moonlight to see where we were going we got home okay.

September 18

Today we cleaned and split all the fish that we had caught. Len and Mark made a 10 x 10 smokehouse and we put heavy chicken wire on the outside to keep the bears out. We put the fish over wood poles. We made a fire out of alders and driftwood from the beach and smoked about 200 salmon. We packed some of the fish whole in plastic and boxes and took them to the cannery freezer. We put some fish in a couple barrels of salt brine so we can pickle some of the salmon. It took us all day to finish working with the fish. We were tired by evening.

We had salmon, rice and berries for dinner. We also took some fish eggs and boiled them and mixed them with mayonnaise, and Worcestershire sauce, it was so good.

Last night the dogs were barking and we shined the flashlight out the window and could see two big mean looking bears trying to get into the smoke house. Their eyes glowed red when the light from the flashlight shown on them. When they saw the light they ran away. The smokehouse is only about 20 feet from our house.

September 19

Len's uncle said he would help him build a skiff. We will pay him five hundred dollars next fishing season since he is supplying the plywood and oak. It is so nice to be with Len and have him home. He played his guitar and sang songs to me tonight.

Ashley gave us her feather mattress to put on top of our other one, which is so hard without springs. I see why she gave it away. The feathers move around at night when you turn over and it isn't under you anymore. I think we will give it away.

September 20

Today a cargo and passenger boat came into the bay to bring supplies for the winter. Len was surprised to see his two cousins, Kyle and Rosie, and his aunt Carole, come ashore. His cousin Kyle is about his age and Rosie is a very pretty 15 year old.

Kyle is Len's best friend and they were glad to see each other again. He will be helping Kyle fix up an old house that no one lives in about a half mile from us. The family will stay there while Carole's boyfriend fishes for king crab somewhere by Kodiak. Len said he would give some fish and moose meat to them. They came to our house to visit and had dinner with us. They are staying at Mark's tonight because he has a bigger house than we do.

September 21

This morning Len and I went to help his aunt and cousins fix up their house.

Rosie answered the door and I was kind of embarrassed because she was in her pajama top and you could see right through it like she had nothing on. It didn't seem to bother her. She walked around that way and she didn't get dressed for about an hour. The house is in pretty bad shape and needs a lot of work. We went home in the afternoon.

Len said Kyle and Carole were making a barrel of beer out of canned fruit, sugar, yeast and potatoes. They are going to have a party later this week, and invited him.

I'm not used to being around drinking parties, my parents

did not drink and I never have. Len told me when we got married that he didn't drink and I hope Kyle doesn't talk him into drinking. I don't think he is going to be a good influence on Len. He gave him a bunch of naked girlie magazines to take home. I was pretty upset about it but he made it very clear he is going to look at them whether I like it or not.

September 22

Len's uncle came over around noon and they started making the 16-foot skiff. I went down to the beach and watched them make it. It was really interesting. They did a good job and made the sides higher than most of the other skiffs, so it could hold a lot of fish.

September 23

Today we went to the village and picked up old outboard motor parts that people had thrown away. He is going to assemble an outboard motor for the skiff. We put all the outboard motor parts we had found in the village on the kitchen floor. With him telling me what to do I helped him put them together and he assembled a 45-horsepower outboard motor. It worked as well as a new one when he was finished. I was really proud of him. Now we can give Chris's outboard motor and skiff back to him.

He played his guitar and sang to me, and then we read the Bible and went to bed.

September 24

I made breakfast from some of the smoked salmon that wasn't completely smoked yet. I put it in the oven and baked it. It was really good that way. The salmon we salt-brined for pickling won't be ready for a while yet. When it is ready Len told me to put it in an empty sugar sack and tie it to an alder bush by the creek and let it hang in the water for a day to wash out all the salt. Then put it in a jar and add pickling spices for a while. He said it is really good if you like pickled fish.

September 25

We visited Len's uncle who lives close by and is 90 years old. He told us when he was younger he and some other men had been out hunting and found a gold-colored rock. When they camped that night they put the rock in a pan over the campfire and it melted and coated the bottom of the pan. He said the rock might have been gold. He also told us stories about the village a long time ago.

This village used to have a large population until some natives in the village ate a whale, and they turned blue and died, leaving only about half the people alive. He said the Russians came one year and took a lot of the young women away for slaves. The men tried to stop the Russians but were overpowered and a lot of men were killed. He said the Japanese also came and took some of the village woman and killed some men. He said there were only about 2,000 Aleuts left on the Aleutian Chain and most of them are a quarter or half Russian.

October 30

Someone gave Len some western pocket books and he wants me to read to him at night. He falls asleep while I am reading and if I quit reading he wakes up. I want to go to sleep and turn off the lamp but when I try to he gets mad and he pulls the hairs on my arm to keep me awake. It really hurts. If I tell him that, he gets mad at me. I hope the lamp will go out of gas and he will let me go to sleep.

October 31

Tonight Ashley's children came dressed up for Halloween and came to our house trick or treating. They had their faces painted up and paper hats on. They were so cute, and I gave them some cookies.

November 1

The neighbor children got a puppy. Len was outside and tried to pet it but it was scared of him and nipped him. He hit the puppy on the nose and killed it. When he told me I felt so sorry for the puppy. He took it, put it in a sack and buried it in the sand so the neighbors wouldn't know. I don't think he meant to kill it. I am beginning to see he has a very bad temper.

November 2

We saw some little baby feral kittens today and made a box trap to catch them and put some food in it. It wasn't long before an orange striped one and a grey striped one went inside and we pulled the string and shut the door to the trap. We took the box inside the house and opened the door. They were so scared they ran straight up our walls. We made them a bed and gave them some canned milk. We made them a little sand box. I'll have to keep them inside for a while until they get tame. They are so cute and are both little males. They don't seem to be afraid of the dog and she leaves them alone.

I don't know why Len is so mean to them. Maybe because he can't make them mind him. He gets mad at them and throws them against the wall. I feel so sorry for them. I'm afraid he will hurt them. He has such a bad temper sometimes.

Kyle came to our house about 8:00 p.m. and wanted Len to come over for a party. The keg of beer he had made was ready. I asked him to please not go but he wouldn't listen to me. I tried to go outside to talk to him but he shoved me inside and locked me in. I really hated being locked inside my house. He didn't come home tonight. I was up all night and couldn't sleep.

November 3

Len came home in the late morning. I had just broken out a window pane. I was trying to get out of the house when he came in. I had been worried about him and was glad he was okay even though I was mad at him. I told him he better not ever lock me in again. I can't believe he stayed there all night drinking. I didn't want to say much because he had Kyle with him. He said they came to get the shotgun and were going out duck hunting.

Around noon Carole came to the door. I let her in and she said she wanted to visit to get to know me better. I think she was still drunk. She was visiting me for about an hour before she said she had slept with my husband last night. I have never been so hurt in my life. It was like she had stabbed me in the heart with a knife. She had said it like it was nothing, like someone would say I washed clothes today or something. My mouth must have dropped open. I didn't know what to say, I just said she had better go home now because I had work to do.

When she left I cried my eyes out. Why would he go to bed with an old lady who was his aunt? She wasn't even nice looking. Didn't he love me anymore? I couldn't understand what I had done wrong. I did everything for him because I loved him so much. He made love to me three times every day and seemed to enjoy it. How can you make love to someone else if you already love someone? I could never do that. Maybe when we got married he thought he loved me, but maybe he doesn't really love me. I don't know what to do, I am so scared. I would leave him but I don't have the money for airfare and neither do my parents or relatives. I was so mad at him but I had dinner ready for him when he came home. Kyle was with him and ate with us. I wonder if Kyle knows about Len and his aunt. After Kyle left I told him what Carole said and asked him if it was true. I started crying and asked him if he didn't love me anymore. He said yes he still loved me, but that's what the men here did and if I didn't like it that was too bad. He said one woman would never be enough for him.

I felt like ending my life so I wouldn't have to stand the hurt anymore. I took about twenty aspirin and swallowed them. He found out and didn't really care, he just got mad and that made me mad so I threw up the pills. I prayed to God for forgiveness for trying to commit suicide.

He said he was going back to the party again tonight. As he was leaving I begged him not to go but he didn't listen. I finally got to sleep about one in the morning.

I'd been trying to figure out what to do. I realized I made a bad mistake marrying him without knowing him longer. I'm really mad about this. It's so unfair. I read my Bible a lot and prayed to God about my marriage. I know the Bible says to forgive and that love and marriage are forever, unless the person you are married to is unfaithful. I was so glad I had God to talk to, it was such a comfort. I wish my mother lived closer to me.

November 4
I woke up this morning feeling terrible. He hadn't come

home yet. I held my dog in my arms and cried. I decided I wasn't going to stay here any longer with him. I packed a small hand bag with my Bible, some of my pictures and my mom's letters and started walking the two miles to the cannery. I had to walk on the beach by the house where he was drinking. I was so afraid he might see me and try to stop me.

I went to the village where the missionaries from Australia lived. They were staying in a small house in the village. I was afraid they might not let me stay with them.

When I got to their house they were having lunch and invited me to join them. I told them I was having a problem with my husband and asked if I could stay with them for a while until I could find a way to get out of here. I told them what he did and I wanted to go home to my parents and get a divorce.

I was so relieved when they said yes and were so nice that I started to cry. They were so kind and said I could stay there. I was so glad they took me in. I went to bed in their spare room and I fell right asleep as I was so tired.

November 5

This morning after breakfast Len came to the missionary's door and told them he wanted to talk to me. I didn't want to but they said I should talk to him because he said he loved me and seemed really upset. He wanted me to go home with him. I was still hurt and mad at him and felt he didn't love me. I really didn't want to see him. I finally went to the door and he wanted me to come outside and talk to him so I did. He said he was sorry, he would never do anything like that again and that he loved me and he didn't want me to leave him.

He tried to pull me into his arms but I pulled away. He started crying. I felt so sorry for him. It was terrible to see him cry. I told him I would go home with him but I was still mad at him, and if he ever did anything like that again I would leave him. I put my things back in my small overnight bag and I thanked the missionary and we went back home. I would just try and forget everything and go on from here. I don't like him very much right now, maybe later I will be able to forgive him.

It's just like he killed some of the love and trust and respect I had for him. I don't know if I'll ever have the same kind of love for him.

November 10

He asked me this morning if I would like to go to Kodiak with him and work in the cannery this winter. There are crab and shrimp canneries there that need workers. I really liked the idea. I had worked in canneries before in Washington. It would be better than staying here all winter with nothing to do and no money and not enough food to eat. An airline in Dillingham said they would let us charge the airfare to Kodiak and we could pay him later. We still had some money left from fall fishing. We would have to leave for Kodiak at the end of November. Len said it will be hard to get a place to rent. No apartments were available and there were only two old hotels there. We can't afford to rent a house. He said we would find something. We will have to board up the windows on our house before we leave. I'm so excited, it will be fun to work again and be in a town even if it is only a one street town. I will be able to go to church again.

November 20

This morning we started making plans to leave. We stocked up on staples and put them into tin cans in the attic so we would have something to eat as soon as we got back without going to the store right away. We chopped lots of wood and bought some gas for the lantern. I made bread and we went hunting for ducks for supper.

About 11 pm I heard a knock at the door. I hadn't been able to fall asleep but he was sleeping hard so I didn't wake him and I went to the door. It was Carole and she was drunk and wanted to see Len. I told her he was sleeping. She said she wanted him to come to her place and make love to her. We were both standing on the porch and I just got so mad and punched her in the face. She was knocked off the porch with my blow and I hit her again, I was so mad. I had never gotten that mad at anyone before. Then I calmed down and felt so bad because I had hit her and given her a bloody nose. She asked me what was wrong with me. I told her I was sorry and to please just go back home. I'm going to be so glad to leave here. I crawled back in bed without waking him up. I'm not going to tell him what happened, he would probably be mad at me. I felt so bad that I hit her.

November 24

My Cocker Spaniel had puppies. They were so cute and it was the first time I had seen anything born. Len told me to put them in a gunny sack and drown them. I said I wasn't going to do that. Then he doubled up his fist and threatened to hit me and I got scared and put them in the gunny sack and waded into the bay with them. I was crying and I dropped the bag in but I hadn't tied the top and they all came out trying to swim so I picked them all up and took them back into the house. I got mad at him and said I wasn't going to drown them, I would find homes for them. I dried them off and they were okay. Ashley took one of them and the natives in the village took some and I was so glad. He didn't say anything more about it.

November 25

Mark said he would take care of our dog and cats for us while we were gone.

We left for Kodiak in a big float plane that had pontoons and landed on the water. It was really frightening when we landed because the plane sank so low into the water. The water level came up over the windows before the plane came back up to the surface.

Kodiak was a small town with only one main street and a big sea port. It is pretty here with the snow-capped mountains in view behind the little town. The main road is gravel and has a small supply store, and grocery store, two churches (one was Russian Orthodox), a clothing store, two hotels, and a lot of bars. There is also a Navy base here.

We rented a room at an old hotel about two blocks away from the cannery where we will be working. We have to share a toilet at the end of the hall. The room has one bed, an oil range stove, a table and refrigerator. We are going to try to get work right away if we can. Today we will buy groceries on credit. It is great to have electricity again. We can wash clothes at a laundry mat in town. It's pretty cold here already.

December 1

Today we both got jobs in the king crab cannery. Len works where they butcher the crab and then throw them on a moving belt where crab meat comes in piles to be put into cans. I work with a lot of women. It is fun, and I enjoy visiting with the women as we work. They all talk a lot about the good and mostly bad times with their husbands and don't seem to mind who hears them talk about their personal sex life. We make good money, $4.50 an hour. We work long hours and get overtime pay. At the end of the day we can take home any king crab meat left on the tables. We make salads or fry the legs in butter.

I wanted to go to church but Len got so mad at me when I told him, that I was too scared to go. He said if I went to the church he would drag me out by my hair. It really upset me

47

that I had the opportunity now to go to church but he wouldn't let me.

I was hoping we would save some money but Len started playing the pinball machines at a restaurant and put everything we made into them. He is so addicted to them and put so much of our money in them we hardly have enough money to buy food and pay rent. He makes me sit for hours watching him. It is so boring and I hate it, but I don't say anything to him. I know he will get mad at me.

I was tired from working all day and wanted to go to our room to rest. He would make me stay with him until midnight or until he ran out of money. I needed shoes as mine had fallen apart and I had to wear small thin rubber boots with socks in them with no lining and they weren't very warm. I could feel the concrete through them.

He lost all our money one night and told me to go outside and beg for money for him. I told him no! He got so crazy mad and I was scared he was going to hit me so I went outside and asked a man for some change. I was so embarrassed. He gave me a few quarters. I was mad and went in and told him to never ask me to do that again or I would leave him. He never did ask me to again.

December 24

We had to work today in the cannery, even though it is Christmas Eve. It was nice though because all of us women sang Christmas songs while we worked. The town was decorated for Christmas and we got each other a small gift. It was snowing and very pretty, and not cold as the winters in Washington. I made a nice dinner with the crab from the cannery. I do miss my family a lot.

A young couple from our village who married about a year ago had a baby. They came to Kodiak to work at the cannery too. Her husband became addicted to pinball machines also and lost all of their money. I felt so sorry for her. She came to me one day for some money to buy milk for her baby and I only had a few dollars to give her.

I was wondering why I wasn't pregnant yet. I loved children

48

and wanted a baby so much but there were times I didn't think it would be good to have children because Len had such a terrible temper. I talked to him about not being able to get pregnant. He said when he was young he hurt his hip and had to have surgery. They used radiation and didn't shield him so he might be sterile. He said he didn't like children and if I ever had a baby and it cried he would leave me. I was really shocked. I know he never played with or talked to any children in the village, but I never knew he didn't want any. I had always wanted children.

1962
April

We had been in Kodiak about six months. In a couple of months it would be time for the men in the village to start getting the boats and seines ready for the June fishing season. Len didn't want to work anymore and he wanted to quit and go home. I wanted to stay and work, I didn't want to go back to the village yet.

Today he told me to quit working, we were going home. He had talked to a pilot that had a small Cessna plane that could take us to the village. The next day we were about to board the plane when two of Len's relatives saw us and yelled at us to come with them, they had chartered a plane that was a little bigger. Len didn't want to tell them no so he said okay. We took our luggage off the little plane with the pilot and two passengers on board. When the Cessna took off it hit an air pocket and couldn't lift off the ground high enough to clear a pile of gravel at the end of the runway. The plane hit it and blew up and caught on fire. It was so terrible to see, it really scared me. I stood there in shock! All of the three people on the plane died. I felt so sorry for them. I don't know why God spared us, but I was very thankful. It could have been us on that plane. I will never forget this.

When we got home I went to get my dog from Len's brother Mark. He said my dog had gotten sick and died. Mark felt bad about it. He said he couldn't get it to eat. I never knew the dog would miss me that much and not eat. I really loved my dog.

When Len was mad at me and I was scared of him, I would hold the dog in my lap out on our porch and cry. She was such a comfort, I will miss her so much. I had so much fun with her. The cats had gone wild when we left. When they saw we were home they came back to the house. Besides Mark feeding them they must have been eating rats under the wood pilings. They were really big and fat. It was so good to see them again.

April

I went to the village store today to get a few groceries. A woman told me the village had a council meeting and had made the missionaries and Carole leave the village. The missionaries and Carole were causing so much trouble. They were going from house to house and gossiping about everyone. The missionaries had told everyone about Carole sleeping with my husband. It was hard for me to believe they would do that.

The weather is not so cold but there is still no sun out and there is snow on the ground. It is Easter and I really miss going to church to worship on Easter with my family. I made Russian Easter Bread. I put an egg in the bread mixture and rolled the dough out and put cinnamon and brown sugar and raisins on it and rolled up the dough and put it inside of a coffee can and baked it. When it had cooled, I put icing on top of the bread. It was really good.

May

Today Len and Mark went out hiking for grouse and found a baby bird, a little magpie. It was all alone and couldn't fly yet. They caught it and brought it home to me. I made a pen for it out of fishing net and put it inside our porch. In a couple of weeks it was tamed and eating out of my hand. It was so cute. It would wake me up at three in the morning, which wasn't so cute. It would be crying wanting to eat but I really didn't mind. I would feed it some fish and go back to sleep.

This morning I woke up at three out of habit to feed the little bird but it wasn't crying. I was worried about it and hurried out to the porch to see what was wrong. It was so sad when I saw what had happened. It had managed to get its head through one of the holes in the fishing net and when it tried to get its head out it couldn't and he broke his neck. I feel so bad about it. I really liked my little pet bird.

June 24

A relative of Len's gave us their gas washing machine. I was glad to get it but it needs to be worked on. You have to pull out a cord on it to start it like you do on the outboard motors. It never wants to start. I have to try about a half hour to get it going. I hope Len can fix it. It will be better than washing on a washboard.

June 25

We saw a big gray wolf dead along the edge of the water today. It's the first wolf we have ever seen here. I wonder if someone shot it or if it died some other way.

They went out fishing today and there is a big run of salmon. Some men that live in the village about 15 miles from us have new fiberglass boats. The boats are faster and they have 75 H.P. motors on their skiffs. They can get to the fish faster than the other fishermen. A couple of them also have small planes and can go and see where the fish are running. They are called High Liners because they make about $150,000 in 21 days after paying their crew. Usually there are just four men on a 26-foot boat. Other fishermen make about $21,000 to $30,000.

The season is really good and the Alaska Packers Cannery here needs more workers to keep up with canning all the incoming fish before they go bad. Len let me go to work in the cannery. I work in the can shop, making cans for the women to put the fish in. I really like working, and the native women I work with from the village are really nice. One time the fish run was so big we had to work for two days and two nights without going home to sleep.

June 26

Today the wind was so strong I couldn't take the skiff to work. That night I had to walk along the beach to go home. There was a full moon and it was so light out that you didn't need a flashlight. The stars seemed so close and it seemed like you could almost reach up and touch them. There were so many of them, it was really pretty! God made such a beautiful world for us to live in!

Len bought me a 45 pistol for short range. I wore it in a holster on my hip in case a bear jumped out at me from the bank onto the beach, when walking home from work.

June 27

Late this afternoon a big storm came up fast and the men were out fishing. Ashley's husband had just bought a new 45 H.P outboard motor and had put it on his skiff. It was anchored out in the water. The wind was blowing so hard and the waves were so big the skiff was starting to sink. I waded out to my waist in the water and was able to get in the skiff. I had to hold my breath and put my head in the water to be able to unloosen the clamps on the outboard motor from the skiff. I lifted it out of the skiff and dragged it onto the beach. Ashley and I got some cardboard and put the motor on it and dragged it up the beach above the tide line. I was so glad it didn't get wet and ruin it. The tide went out and we bailed the skiff out and put some long round driftwood under it and with the kids' help we were able to get it up on the beach above the water line.

June 30

Tonight I walked home from the cannery on the beach. It was really dark out and I had to use a big flashlight. I heard a noise on the bank and I could see in the flashlight beam two bears watching me. Their eyes looked red in the light. I was afraid but I sang one of my favorite songs, "Anywhere with Jesus I Can Safely Go". I thanked God they didn't attack me, and I got home okay. I didn't want to have to shoot them. The cannery had thrown all the egg roe and innards of the fish into the bay and it washed ashore and the smell from the fish brought the bears around. I will be glad when the wind quits blowing so hard, so I can take the skiff to work.

I was so happy I was working and making some money. When Len came in from fishing he would play poker in the village with other men and lose money, but not very much. Some of the men gambled $1,000 on a single hand of poker and would lose all their money.

Sept

He made $2,500 fishing this summer and with what I made in the cannery we were able to pay his uncle for building the skiff for us. We paid our grocery bill with Alaska Packers and we were also able to buy some plywood for the walls. We painted it with varnish. We bought some linoleum for the floor and heavy gauge tin for the roof and some Plexiglas. Len is going to make a big window in the kitchen and use Plexiglas so the bears can't break in. We bought a small oil stove for the bedroom and an oil cooking range for the kitchen. Len kept enough money for us to go on the ferry boat to Kodiak. It had never came to the village before. He wanted us to work in the cannery there again.

November

We left for Kodiak on the ferry today. It had passengers on it and cargo. It was fun being on a ferry boat. We had to cross the Shelikof Straits which are known for storms and rough water. We got caught in a big storm with really strong winds. The boat was rolling a lot from side to side, almost tipping over. It was late afternoon and we were told to lie down in our beds. The crew had set up two cots for us in the galley. We kept rolling off of our cots. I got really seasick. The captain had run out of seasick pills. Everyone was seasick, even the captain. I managed to make it outside and threw up over the side of the boat, with Len hanging onto me.

The captain had tried to drop anchor to help stabilize us but the water was too deep for the anchor to touch bottom. Everyone was really scared the ferry was going to sink. I prayed that we would make it through the storm okay. I think God was with the captain and us because the wind died down after an hour and we made it to Kodiak.

We are staying at the same hotel as before. We are working in the same cannery again and at the same jobs as before. A boat that had a load of king crab was delayed because of the bad weather and couldn't get into the cannery before the crab died. Crab canned 24 hours after they have died are not suitable for canning and eating.

A Japanese boat heard about the crab and wanted the cannery to not throw the crab away but can it anyway. They said they would buy them from the cannery and take them to Japan and sell them. The cannery workers heard about it and we all refused to work and went on strike. We thought it was awful that they didn't want to kill people in the U.S. but would sell it to Japan where people would get sick or die from eating it. So the cannery dumped the bad crab. We went to work again when another boat came in with good crab on it.

The union came to the cannery and wanted us all to join. No one wanted to. The cannery said if we didn't join we would lose our jobs. We all joined and had to pay a fee of $50 dollars. The people working in the office all took off to Mexico with the money. The union didn't make us pay again.

The union made the men throw the crab on the belt after being butchered twice as much as before. The cans of crab came down the lines so fast us women could not keep up. It was a big mess of crushed cans. They had to slow it back down. We also could not talk to each other while we worked or sing at Christmas anymore.

Len still played the pinball machines after work to my dismay. I wish we had a TV then maybe he would want to stay in our room at night more. This winter we had really cold weather.

We went down to the fishing docks this afternoon. The crab boats had come in all full of thick ice on the sides of the boat and on the deck. Another boat got so loaded down with ice that it sank and everyone on board died. I felt so sorry for their wives. They were at the dock crying and talking to the men on the other boats that made it back to town.

All of a sudden there was a huge meteor shower that looked like all the stars were falling out of the sky. It was so awesome to see. I had never seen anything like that before.

1963

Len wasn't playing pinball machines as much as before. He liked to go play bingo.

We were having fun together playing bingo once a week, we didn't spend much money and sometimes we a won prize. We had been working about five months and then his cousin Kyle came to town. Len went out drinking with him and didn't come home at night until late. Today he didn't come back to the hotel or tonight either.

Today a native couple who I knew from the village came to see me. They told me that they saw Len and Kyle, they were drunk and had gone back to our village. He said to tell me he would send for me later. They were really nice to me and I could tell they felt sorry for me. Len makes me so mad, he could at least have told me he was going. I will have to make enough money to pay the rent and buy food. We had paid the rent for this month and I could pay the rent the next month but wouldn't have any money for food. I was scared and went to a small grocery store and they gave me credit and I will pay them with my next check.

I called the church in town and was hoping to get to go to church now. I also was hoping I could talk to someone about my situation and see if they could help me in any way. A lady answered the phone and said she would come to the hotel and talk to me. When she saw me she got really mad and she said I know who you are! I had never seen her before. She said are you pregnant? I told her no. She was yelling and really mad, and I didn't know why, but she was scaring me. She said you are that stripper that works in town. I was really shocked and hurt. I told her I wasn't a stripper and that she was mistaking me for someone else. She didn't believe me and said she would tell the church not to help me and left. I had been told before by a lady where I worked in the cannery that I looked like a twin to a stripper in town. So I knew why she had made a mistake. I was so hurt and cried when she left.

I prayed and read the Bible a lot, but didn't go to church.

May

I hadn't heard from Len and I was getting worried about what to do. I was having a hard time making enough money to pay rent. The king crab season was coming to an end and our hours were cut a lot. I didn't have enough money for next month's rent.

I saw Len's cousin today. I explained my situation to her and she said I could come and stay with them in the one bedroom apartment they were renting. They would try to get in touch with him by shortwave radio. They said I could sleep on the kitchen floor. Her cousin was staying with them and sleeping on the living room sofa. I was very grateful to them. I was so tired from working all day that I fell right to sleep with my clothes still on. I haven't been sleeping well at night.

I went to work and when I came home they said Len had talked to a pilot of a small float plane that was going to our village and he would let me charge the airfare to go home. She said Len and his cousin Kyle had been drinking and partying a lot. I really hated to go back to the village but I felt I had no choice. I wish I had the money to go to my family in Washington but I didn't and I knew my family didn't either. I had nowhere else to go so I flew back to our village the next day.

Len was not there when I got off the plane. The plane landed in the bay at the village cannery in front of the store. A relative of Len's said he was at his aunt and uncle's and they were all drunk. When I got to the house he was with his aunt in a bedroom. I ran out and went to our house. I was so hurt I thought he would be glad to see me after a couple of months apart.

I walked home along the beach the two miles to our shack. What a mess the house was. I started cleaning everything up. Len came home drunk. He was angry and wanted me to cook. I was scared of him so I did. I asked him why he left me in Kodiak without telling me he was going back home. He said he didn't want to work anymore, and that's all he would say. I wish I could have gotten help from the church. I would never have come back here.

June

When we woke up this morning a cargo ship was stuck in the sand right in front of our house by the bank. The tide was high last night and the wind was blowing really hard. It must have dropped anchor in the night and when the tide went out it got stuck. When the tide came in some boats came from the village and pulled it back into the bay.

Len's uncle came back to the village today with a new bride. She is an Eskimo and very nice, I am so happy for them.

Today Mark wanted to know if Len and I would fish with him this summer. He said he would let me cook and run the snag skiff and help on deck again like last time. Len told him we would go with him. I was really glad as I like fishing.

When we were out fishing today, it rained really hard all day. I was running the snag skiff and even with heavy raincoats and hip boots on and I was soaking wet. The fish were really running in schools a lot. I just had time to have a can of beans thrown to me as I went by the boat to eat in the skiff. I had to keep a small hook shape in the end of the seine so the salmon would not follow the net around and get out. When they hit a net that was curved at the end they went right back in the seine again. I also used a long plunger to scare the fish back in the net.

This was all very hard to do because of the strong winds and the pull of the tide. If the fish were jumping out of the water a lot that meant there was a big school of fish in the net. I would close my end of the net around them after they were trapped inside and take the end to the boat so they could be loaded aboard. I had to keep the net taut so it wouldn't go slack and get caught in the boat propeller. I went on deck then and helped stack leads and corks. After fishing I cooked one of the salmon we had caught and had it for dinner. I really like fishing. It is a lot of work but fun and exciting.

July 14

Today our net snagged on a rock and it got caught up in the net. I was on deck running the power block full speed while Len and Mark pulled on the net hard to try to break loose the rock so they could bring the net in. The rock broke loose and shot through the air really fast. I had my head down and never saw the rock coming. It happened so fast. The rock was about a foot long and wide and it hit me on the side of the head by the temple. It picked me up off my feet and threw me to the end of the boat about 10 feet. I had a hard time not passing out. It seemed like I was in a long black tunnel. I knew I had almost died and was trying hard to not black out.

Len brought a bucket of water which was ice cold. He dipped a towel in it and kept putting it on my head. It kept me from passing out. He said he was sorry that happened to me. They took me home and I had a hard time walking straight. I kept seeing double. I thanked God that I was still alive.

Tonight I had to sleep on my back. If I lay on my side I can feel my skull moving. I know it is cracked. I had to drink soup through a straw because my jaw also got hit and wouldn't open far enough to eat. I could feel my skull was crushed in at my temple. We called the hospital in Anchorage on the village shortwave radio but they said not to come there because there were no head doctors there at the time and that I probably had a concussion.

I had to go out fishing today even though I was still dizzy. They had me put on a helmet. I was the only one available that knew how to run the snag skiff for fishing. We had to fish while they were coming into the bay. We needed the money to live on through the winter.

August 31

We finished the summer and fall fishing season. I still have to lie on my back only because of my skull being cracked. It isn't healed yet and I can still feel my skull moving if I lay on my side.

September

The herring are swimming in schools in the bay along the shore. We waded out tonight and caught a lot of them in five gallon buckets. We put a lot of small holes in the bottom of the bucket for the water to run out but still left the herring in the bucket. They are so good fried crispy!

Mark wanted to know if we will go with him to a trapping shack and trap mink with him for the winter. Len told him we would.

October 31

We left the village today to go out trapping. It is about fifteen miles across the ocean by skiff. We can only take staples for food, a cast iron frying pan, a Coleman gas lamp, some white gas, rifles, and traps.

I took the cats with us to catch the mice. I put them in a gunny sack so they wouldn't jump out of the skiff. It is snowing and cold. The small tar paper shack where we are staying has two bedrooms and a kitchen. The place is full of mice. Tonight a mouse ran over my face and I grabbed it and threw it across the room screaming. I hope the cats will start catching them. It is so cold getting up in the morning with no heat. I would get up early and start the fire in the wood stove and jump back into bed until it warms up.

Today I made fried Indian bread and cooked for the men while they were out hunting and checking the traps they had set out. In the evening we worked on the mink skins. We put the skin over a small board and took a table knife and scraped all of the gristle off of the skin very carefully. Then we finished tanning the hides and getting them ready to sell later. It was a lot of work but we needed the money to live on. A couple of times they took me out with them hunting. We had to live off the land because we were 15 miles by boat to any village store. The moose have moved too far inland to find them.

We came across a small pond at the end of a creek with about six salmon in it. Mark shot into the pond with his rifle and it killed them. We will have fish to eat for a few days.

November 22

We heard on the shortwave radio today that President Kennedy died, and that he had been shot. That was really shocking news to us. They didn't have very many details yet. We will listen again later.

1964
March

Len and Mark took me duck hunting with them today and had me run the skiff around and scare the ducks toward them in the bushes so they could shoot them. They yelled at me to pick up the dead ones. One was alive and not hurt too bad, his wing had just been broken. Len yelled at me to wring its neck but I wouldn't. They let me take it with us to the shack.

I put a splint on the duck's wing and kept it in the shed and fed it. After a short time its wing healed and I took it outside and it flew away. I was so happy it could fly again and was okay. They never took me duck hunting again and I was glad! It is early spring and we went back home to the village.

March 27

Len, Mark and I were standing outside of our house today and the ground started rolling under our feet. We knew right away it was an earthquake. It only lasted about a minute. We turned on the shortwave radio and heard that there had been a big earthquake in Anchorage. A tsunami had come and hit Kodiak and other villages. We could hear on our shortwave radio a fisherman out in his boat saying, "Oh my God! There's a 20-foot wave in front of me!" Then not a sound from him and I knew he probably died. It was so sad and it made you wish you could help somehow.

We were warned to go up in the mountains in case of a tidal wave. We were going to go up on the hill behind our house but we changed our mind. We saw all of the water go out of the bay in a couple of minutes and all of the bottom fish were left on the floor of the bay. We went down with pans and picked up halibut and other fish. Thank God the water didn't come back in the bay fast and drown us.

We didn't realize how bad the earthquake was until we went back in the house with the fish. We could hear on the radio all the damage it did everywhere. It was really terrible. When we woke up this morning the water was all back in the bay and we didn't have a tidal wave. The earthquake didn't do any damage in our village. Len's relatives in Anchorage called the village on shortwave radio and told us about the earthquake there. His relatives in Kodiak told us about the tsunami.

One of his cousins in Kodiak had to crawl on her hands and knees to the yard outside to get to her children. The ground was shaking so hard she couldn't stand up. She said she saw people on top of car hoods that were washed out to sea with the tidal wave. Big fishing boats were washed up into the town streets. It was really terrible. Villages were washed away along the coast from the tsunami. In Anchorage, the main street downtown split open and people and buildings fell into the huge crevices. The shortwave radios were filled with people telling what had happened and other people trying to find family and relatives. We heard the earthquake in Anchorage was a 9.2 magnitude.

My mother had called the Red Cross and they sent a message to the village by shortwave radio to see how we were. She was so glad to hear that we were okay. We still had earthquakes of 6.5 magnitude every couple of weeks for the rest of the month.

April

Len's uncle's wife had a baby boy. They live about a mile from us. I am so happy for them.

A young man from the village, who is 16 years old, came to visit us today. We had just got back from hunting and had not emptied our guns yet. We had set our 45 pistol on the table and he picked it up and twirled it on his finger and pulled the trigger. We were very blessed that it was aimed towards the ceiling when it went off. It made a big hole in the ceiling and hurt our ears and scared us but no one was hurt. We really were surprised he pulled the trigger because he was used to handling guns and hunting.

June

Len went out fishing with his brother again this summer. He said they saw a Russian boat close to shore and they shot at it with their rifles. They were mad because they weren't supposed to be fishing so close to our shores. I don't think that was a very good idea. They were lucky they didn't shoot back at them.

I'm not going out fishing this summe will work i cannery, I really like working there with the her women. I w make cans in the can shop again for the sa n to be put in.

Ashley came to see me when I got hom rom work today. They had caught a big groundhog by scooti it with a broom into a box. We looked at it and let it go. It w the first one we had ever seen here. I was just going to light t e oil sto e in the bedroom and had turned on the carburetor t let oil nto the stove to light it, when Ashley came to get me to ee the groundhog. When I went home I didn't think very much oil would be in the stove that quickly. I threw a match in to light it. There must have been quite a lot of oil in the stove. It got so hot the smoke stack from the stove to the ceiling turned red. I got scared and threw some flour in the stove and put it out. What a mess to clean up. I would never do that again. At least the house didn't burn down.

July

Today I was throwing out the anchor to the skiff I was in and it caught on my ring and took my class ring off and almost took my finger off too. Then my nose started bleeding really bad. This is the first time this has happened to me since I was at my parent's home. I used to get nose bleeds a lot as a child. I took the skiff and went to the doctor. It was hemorrhaging and he had to cauterize it. I was so glad it was summer and the doctor was at the village to help me.

September

Len went out fall fishing with Mark for a couple of weeks. Len is back today and they did good fishing.

Len and I went out moose hunting today and saw a bull moose and three other moose by him. They were on a hill real close to the beach. He jumped out of the skiff and shot one of them, and the other two ran away. We cut it up and packed it to the skiff. I felt sorry for it but I am so glad we will have moose for the winter to eat.

November

A couple, who is related to Len, and their 13 year old daughter came from another village to visit us. They wanted to stay overnight and leave the next day on the plane. We let the husband and wife have our bed and Len, the girl, and I had to sleep on the kitchen floor in sleeping bags.

I was sleeping next to the 13 year old. During the night Len woke me up and wanted me to go with him to the porch so he could tell me something. When we got out there he said he wanted me to stay outside and he said he was going to make love to the girl. I got so mad at him and yelled no! He got really mad and grabbed me and shoved me out the door and locked *it*. He really scared me, and I was so worried about the little girl. *I* kicked on the door but he wouldn't let me back in. I prayed *to* God for the little girl that he wouldn't rape her. I didn't know *what* to do. It was so cold out, about 30 degrees, and I just had on *my* sweat pants and sweatshirt. I went to Ashley's house and knocked but they were asleep and didn't hear me. I went to this big *old* house that his brother Mark lived in. He had gone to another village for the winter. It wasn't locked and was empty but there were no blankets or anything to keep warm with, I was so *cold*. I thanked God for some cardboard that I found and put it over *myself*, it would help me to keep me from freezing tonight. I *couldn't* sleep all night.

I had no *place* to go except back to our house the next morning. It was so cold out I needed to get inside the house and get warm. The visitors were all in the bedroom and Len was really mad at *me*. *I* was really mad at him but too scared to say anything to him. My heart was racing and I didn't feel very good. He said he didn't do anything, that the girl must have heard us fighting and went in with her parents. He warned me not to say anything to them. I was so thankful that she didn't get raped. He told me to cook breakfast for them. They didn't talk much, just ate and left. Len went in to the bedroom and went to sleep.

While he was sleeping I left the house with my small overnight case and walked along the beach to the village. I was going to leave him. A plane was coming in this morning and I

63

went to see one of his aunts that had moved here recently from Kodiak. She loaned me money for the airfare to Kodiak. She said she had talked to her daughter in Kodiak on her shortwave radio. Her daughter said she would let me stay with her family in their Quonset hut.

I arrived in Kodiak and she met me at the airport. She and her family were really nice to me. She has a couple of small children. It was the first time I had been in a Quonset hut, they had it fixed up really nice. They let me sleep on the sofa. When it rained it was really loud hitting the tin roof. I got a job working in the shrimp cannery right away. I don't like to impose on them. I hope I can save enough money to go home to my parents soon.

I had been working about a week when I heard Len was trying to find me and had flown into town. His relatives that I was staying with either felt sorry for him or needed the $500 I heard he gave them. They told him where I was working and today he came to my job and wanted to talk to me. I told him no and he got mad and started dragging me out of the building. He asked me to forgive him and said he would never do anything like that again. I didn't believe him but I was so scared of him that I went with him.

He wanted to stay in Kodiak with me and work. He said his cousin would let us stay together in their travel trailer. I don't love him anymore. I wish I could get away from him and get a divorce.

We lived in the travel trailer and it was very uncomfortable. It was so small and we had to use his cousin's bathroom in the Quonset hut. I cooked on the stove and the walls would get wet from the steam and the blanket on the bed against the wall got wet. We stayed in Kodiak for the winter and worked in the shrimp and crab canneries.

1965

April

We flew back home today in a small Cessna plane and we were flying by some cliffs when all of a sudden we were upside down in our seats. I screamed and the pilot said he was sorry but an eagle had dropped down right in front of the plane. He said he had to turn the plane upside down to miss it. He was the best bush pilot on the whole peninsula, and I'm sure I must have a guardian angel watching over me.

May

Len and I went to visit someone at the village today and a cargo ship was in at the dock. I was walking on the dock with him and to my surprise I saw the neighbor boy that I grew up with as a child was on the boat. He was waving to me. I didn't wave back which really made me feel bad. I knew Len would see me waving and really get mad at me, he was so jealous.

Someone from another village brought some puppies to our village and we took one to our house. It was a little male Beagle/German Shepherd mix but was small and looked more like a Beagle. It was so cute. I was so happy to have a puppy again.

Len's brother Chris came back from Sandpoint today. He said he had fallen down a flight of steps and hit his head. He had surgery and the doctors had implanted a metal plate in his forehead. He had come here to go fishing with Len and his brother Mark.

Today Chris, Len and I and a few other people went to a lake about a mile from our house to go swimming. Chris dove into the lake. A man that had been standing by him noticed that he didn't come back up. He swam in to see why and saw Chris underwater not moving by an oil drum, and pulled him ashore. He was unconscious because he had hit his head on the oil drum that someone had put in the lake. His forehead was bleeding quite a bit.

Someone went for the doctor who came in for the summer and had an office in the village. Len and I tried mouth-to-mouth resuscitation and pushed on his chest but couldn't get him breathing again. I felt so sorry for him. The doctor said he had died when his head hit the drum. Len and Mark were really close to Chris and were really hurt by his death. Chris was such a nice person. They buried him on the hill by his dad near the Russian Orthodox Church. They had a nice funeral for him.

They will miss him a lot.

June

The fishing season has started and Len and I went fishing with his brother Mark. I worked in the snag skiff again with one end of the net. I was circling the fish and the net snagged on a rock and I tried to pull it loose. I pulled so hard I finally did get it loose, but I hurt my back. I was in such bad pain that I couldn't sleep at night very much. When I walked I would get a spasm in my back and fall down to my knees.

My back got so bad I couldn't even walk at all. Len carried me to the doctor who was also an Osteopath. He had a business in New York. He said I had damaged a disk in my back and it was pinching a nerve on one side. The doctor worked on my back again today and the neighbor lady went with me. The doctor said he had come to Alaska to get a record moose rack. He had heard about a big Canadian moose that was here. I saw the one he was talking about when we were out hunting. Last fall it was on top of a hill quite far from us and its rack was huge. We never did shoot a moose for the rack or even keep the moose rack.

After working on my back he gave me a muscle relaxant and aspirin and put some wide tape around my back and waist. I could walk again and not fall down or be in pain so bad. He told me not to go fishing anymore but I did because they needed me to run the snag skiff. I will just keep going back to the doctor until the season is over. My back will get better when I quit fishing.

The doctor told us about a man in a village about 12 miles from us who had stabbed his wife in her privates and killed her. The doctor had gone there but couldn't save her. He also told us about a young boy in another village who had shot his mom and dad with a shotgun when he was drunk. The man who killed his wife, and the boy who shot his parents, were in jail a few weeks and then allowed to come back to the village.

September

Mark and Len found someone to go fall fishing with them

and I stayed home.

Big ravens were coming around the house. I thought maybe if I could catch a raven I could have it for a pet. My brother in Washington had a pet crow when we were kids. I used the box trap I had trapped the kittens in and put some salmon in it. The raven went in and was trapped inside. When I opened the box I could see in his eyes how frightened he was. I felt sorry for him and let him go.

November

Winter is here and we have snow already. We went out to the trap shack with Len's brother Mark to hunt for moose. We took the dog and cats with us today. We landed on the beach and pulled the skiff up above the tide line and went to the trap shack. The shack was built into the side of the hill. It had been snowing and we could see bear tracks on the tar paper roof because of the snow. When we got inside we noticed someone had taken the small wood stove. We went down on the beach and found an empty oil drum and rolled it back to the shack. We took it inside and stood it upright and cut a hole in the side big enough to get wood in and placed the cut out piece of metal over the hole. It made a really good stove and I could cook on the top of it. We made a smoke stack out of coffee cans we found washed up on shore and also the empty ones inside the shack. We used drift wood from the beach to put in the stove for firewood.

I saw a white ermine this morning by a stack of old logs. I remember Len's uncle telling us a story about how an ermine came into a trapping shack at night and bit the man sleeping there in the neck and sucked his blood out. I didn't really believe him and I think he was just trying to scare me. I could hear the cats catching the mice tonight.

I went out hunting with them today and we took the dog with us. We came near some alder bushes and all of a sudden a bear stood up in front of us a couple of feet away. It was growling and waving its arms around and really mad. I grabbed the dog and held onto him. It was dangerously close, and it started charging at us. They both shot at it and Len's rifle jammed and Mark shot it. We couldn't tell for sure if it was dead or not because we couldn't see it through the thick alder bushes it had fallen into. We went back to the shack and stayed there the rest of the day.

Today we went out hunting again and went to the area where Mark had shot the bear. It looked like another bear had dug a hole and buried the dead one. Some natives say the bears bury their dead and dig them up later to eat. Others say it is just something they do. We felt bad about it as we never shoot them unless we have to. We came to a little plywood shack the men from the oil company had built and you could see where a bear had torn up part of the roof with its claws and teeth.

By the shack there was a big empty oil drum full of quartz with gold veins running through it. A long time ago there used to be a gold mine near here, but it wasn't worth the money to mine and ship it out.

This morning I heard my dog barking at something in the logs by the shack. I went to see what he was barking at. I saw what I thought were rabbit droppings so I said "go and get it!" I thought we might have some rabbit to eat. He got really excited and was barking and then got really quiet. He came out from under the logs with porcupine quills in his nose. I felt so sorry for him and knew I had to pull them out right away because when his nose swelled up I wouldn't be able to pull them out. He let me pull them all out but I knew it really hurt him.

We went back to the shack and I couldn't find my gloves lined with rabbit fur that my mother had sent to me. I had taken them off to pull the quills from my dog's nose and forgot to pick them up. We went back for them and they were all torn to pieces and there were wolverine tracks all around them. I will have to knit some gloves for the winter.

Len shot the porcupine and we had it for lunch, it tasted just like a pork roast. We kept the quills and would send them to Anchorage as we could use the money from them.

Len and I went out hiking this morning to look for a moose. Mark went in another direction to look for one. We were crossing a lake that was frozen over. We were trying to be careful as we didn't know how thick the ice was. I was following Len and just about to the shore and the ice gave way under me. Len and our dog were on shore and he grabbed me and pulled me out of the freezing cold water. After hiking I didn't feel that cold, because I had wool pants and hip boots on. We didn't see a moose today and neither did Mark.

We all went out hunting together again today and saw a moose. They shot it, and I helped take the guts out, terrible smell! They cut it up and packed what they could back to the shack. I carried the rifles in case a bear came close. We will have to come back for the rest of it later today. We went back and got the rest of the moose, but it took two trips to pack it all to the shack.

Today we were crossing the ocean to go home to the village and a big wave about 15 feet high came up out of the water, but the rest of the ocean was flat and calm. It was about 500 yards away from us. I had never seen anything like that before. We didn't know what caused it. Maybe there was an earthquake on the ocean floor. I was glad no big waves hit the skiff as it was really low in the water, loaded with moose meat.

We got home and hung the moose meat inside the smokehouse so the bears couldn't get to it. Tonight we heard noises and got our big flashlight and saw two big bears by the smokehouse. We banged on a big five gallon can and they ran away.

Today I cut up all the meat and put it in plastic and boxes

to freeze. Len and Mark after fall fishing had built a shed to put boxes of meat in. In the winter like this it was cold enough to keep the meat frozen.

December

We went to visit the family with 13 children today and took them some moose meat. When we got to the house you could see a fire in the upstairs window. We ran in and told them about the fire. Len ran upstairs and a mattress was on fire. He grabbed the cot-sized mattress and threw it out the window. There was enough snow on the ground that it didn't catch anything else on fire. One of the teenage boys was smoking while in bed and had fallen asleep and dropped his cigarette on the mattress.

Len got some advertising in the mail that said if you worked on this big cross word puzzle and got all the answers right you could win a lot of money. We worked on it a couple of months and got bored with it and gave it up.

December 24

It is Christmas Eve and snowing out and very pretty. It is nice to just celebrate Christmas for the real reason, the birth of Jesus Christ. I cooked a duck dinner for us and read the Bible. There are no stores here to buy presents or decorations. And no pine trees to cut and put in the house. I did knit some stocking caps for some of the children and Len. It was a nice Christmas but I miss my family. I sent them a letter on the last mail plane.

1966
April

It's spring and the williwaws that come are like small tornadoes. One hit our smoke house and lifted it up and set it down about six feet from where it had been but didn't break it up.

The postmaster that lived by the village ordered a log cabin kit. The cabin was really big and had two stories. He hired a carpenter from Anchorage to come to the village and build it for him. They didn't use the big spike nails like we did on all of our houses. A williwaw came and hit his house and it blew all apart. It looked like pick-up sticks all over the place. All the men in the village got together and helped him build it back up. The men from the village nailed it together better.

Mark had to put his Labrador dog down today. I felt so sorry for him. The dog was 16 years old and sick. He will really miss his dog as he lives alone.

Ashley came to our house yelling for help today. Her shed had caught on fire. Len took a broom that was nearby and beat out the flames before they got really bad. They had a big oil generator in the shed for electricity. She thinks that a spark hit an oil spot on the floor and caused it. They offered to let us run an extension cord from their house to ours. We thanked them and put a big light bulb on the end of it so now we finally have light without a gas lantern. So nice!

June 15

Today Len was still out fishing with Mark, and I am working in the cannery this year. Tonight I heard Ashley's husband yelling outside by his house when he came home from fishing. It was dark so I grabbed the big flashlight by my bed and shined it out the window. A big bear was right behind him chasing him up the path, towards his house. I shone my light on the bear and it stopped running and stood up and was swinging his arms around. Ashley's husband had enough time to grab a gun from the house and come out and shoot him. We were so thankful he didn't get killed by the bear!

Alaska Packers had built another bunkhouse this spring. They brought in some Filipino women and men here to work in the cannery this summer. The Filipinos eat lunch sitting on the dock and are always so happy and laughing. Alaska Packers also built on the dock a big shed and attached it to the cannery. They are going to pack the eggroll there and sell it to the Japanese instead of throwing it away into the bay.

Today a big cargo ship from Japan docked at the cannery and took the eggroll. A Japanese man went inside the cannery with a clipboard and was measuring the fish. He was studying them and writing down information about the salmon. The fishermen said Alaska Packers should have never let them do that. Now they would be able to figure out where the fish were running out in the ocean and catch them with their big mother boats, before the fish came into our bays.

I had just gotten home from work late this afternoon when Ashley came to my house. Her dog had bit her little boy on the leg really deep. It must have hurt a lot and he was crying hard. He was only four years old. We washed it out and bandaged it up the best we could. She said he teased the dog a lot that was why it bit him. I felt so sorry for the little boy. We took him to the doctor that is here for the summer.

September 8

The salmon are coming into the creek from the bay right by our house now.

My little dog loves to go in the creek and try to catch them. Once in a while he will catch one. He will keep it in his mouth until he brings it out of the creek. Then he puts it down on the sandy beach and digs a hole and will bury it. I don't know why he thinks he has to store up food as he gets so much to eat.

Len and I went out hunting for moose, and we saw some caribou up on the hill. That is the first time we have ever seen them here. They were pretty far away but Len had bought a high powered rifle. He was able to shoot one of them even at such a far distance. I helped him pack it to the skiff but it was hard to do as it was so far from the skiff and beach. I cooked up some caribou this week but I think the moose meat tastes a lot better. At least we will have meat for the winter again.

He bought a big book on guns and ordered some gun stock wood and is going to put together a rifle and carve a bear on the stock. He also ordered some gun powder to make his own bullets.

September 12

We took our dog in the skiff with us today. We pulled into a little bay and went ashore. We found an old abandoned shack with newspaper on the walls to keep out the cold. I started reading them and they were about Jesse James and other news that happened a long time ago. I took them down without tearing them and rolled them up and took them home.

We also found some fossils on rocks on the beach and green glass balls that came from the Japanese fishing boat seines. The school teacher in our village asked if he could have the newspapers so I gave them to him. In the evening he was teaching the older natives how to read and write and do math.

He finally gave up because a few of them would come in drunk all of the time and disrupt the class.

The school teacher and some people in the village had found some huge footprints of a man today. They were in the wet sand on the beach above the tide line. I was at the store and saw them myself. The teacher made a plaster print of them. They were a lot bigger than any normal man's footprints. Of course some people thought it was Bigfoot. Some people in the village north of us said they had seen a big hairy man in their shed one afternoon and he ran away.

A mail plane came in today and we got the Geiger counter we had ordered in the catalog to hunt for gold. It's very complicated to work. We buried some quarters in the sand on the beach. We went back to the house and got the Geiger counter to find the money but we couldn't. I don't think we are working it right, and we can't figure it out. I don't think we'll be finding any gold with it.

September 15

Mark didn't want to fish the last week of fall fishing. He let Len take the boat out and I went with him and his cousin Kyle, who had just come back to the village. We left at three in the morning and we went along the coastline a long ways from our village. We didn't see any fish because it was so late in the season.

Kyle wanted to go across the ocean to another village and visit some of his relatives. Len said okay and we visited there a while. It was getting late in the afternoon when we started back across the ocean to the other shore. We had been traveling for quite some time when a heavy fog came in fast and we couldn't see where we were going. Our boat had no radar. I could tell they were both scared and so was I. Kyle wanted to go in another direction. Len wouldn't listen to him and kept going straight in the same direction by not turning the wheel a lot. After about a half hour we could see the outline of the land, and followed close to the coastline to get home.

God was really with us. I was so thankful we didn't get lost in the ocean.

October 1

Len has been so good to me these last two years I think he has really changed.

We flew in a small plane to King Salmon today and went on to Anchorage on a jet plane. We took our dog with us as we are going to go see my parents in Washington. I told the airport attendants in King Salmon to be sure and not lose my dog in his dog kennel.

When we got to Anchorage we went to get our dog and they couldn't find him. I was upset, I really love my dog. The airline told us they would call us when they found him. We stayed with Len's sister and family, and it was good to see them again. The airline called us the next day and said they found the dog, and that it had been flown to Japan. They said the dog was okay. The airline attendants could hear him barking in the baggage compartment and that is how they found him. They flew him to Anchorage and we picked him up. We were so glad to see each other!

We rented a car and as we drove through town a lot of the damage from the earthquake was still evident. We started our drive down the Alaska Highway, or Alcan Highway, to Bellingham, Washington. It will be about a 2,700 mile trip. Our dog sat on my lap most of the way. The roads are in really bad shape. The roads haven't been paved yet and are just gravel and some have huge potholes.

It was a long distance between service stations, and we could just make it from one station to the next before we ran out of gas. It was nice to see all the pretty trees with fall colors. I had missed that where we live now. We saw the Northern lights tonight, it was the first time I had seen them. It was so beautiful with such pretty pastel colors.

There were a few souvenir shops for tourists along the road. They made key chains with bear claws on them and bear teeth. The few times we had to shoot a bear we never kept the claws or teeth or hide. It took us two weeks to get to Washington and we are tired.

October 14

It is so good to see my family after six years. We get to be with them for two weeks. We are staying with them at their house. My younger brothers and sister had grown so much in six years. We were all so happy to see each other. My sister let us stay in her room and she slept on the sofa. My family used to live in the country but have moved to the city now.

I never did tell my mother about the bad things in my marriage, and my husband being unfaithful to me. He had been good to me for two years now and I don't think he will ever do things like that again. I didn't want to worry her as she had enough worries of her own. My father had hurt himself at the mill and couldn't work. They were having a hard time. Today my mother got a house cleaning job for someone and I helped her, and could visit with her at the same time. She has bursitis in her arm and is in pain. I feel so sorry for her. I told her I could do it myself but she wanted to help some. The two weeks went so fast and I hate to leave. I love her and the rest of my family so much.

October 15

We started our long trip back to Anchorage today and we saw some dead wolves along the road that had been hit by trucks or cars. We had been on the road a few days and it is cold, winter is setting in fast. When we got to Whitehorse in the Yukon Territory of Canada, a snow blizzard came in and you could hardly see the icy road. We started sliding towards the edge of the cliff where there are no guard rails or shoulder. I was ready to jump out of the car but he got it straightened out in time so we didn't go over the cliff. I was so scared and thanked God that we made it back on the road okay.

When we finally came to a small hotel that night they said they were filled up and there was no room. We asked if we could just stay in the lobby if we paid and they said no, we had to leave. We had to start driving again.

From the blizzard being so bad cars were in the ditch along the road. Len had to drive really slowly to stay on the road. He drove for 24 hours without sleep before we came to a motel that had a room. There was a service station there and we bought some chains for the tires.

We got outside the city of Anchorage and were in another storm. The highway was paved but icy, and the road was slanted. On curves the car would slide and he would have a hard time staying on the road. We had to get gas again and the man at the service station said Len had put the chains on backwards and the spikes were against the tires. The tires were ruined and we had to get new ones.

We finally arrived in Anchorage safely. We stayed with his sister that night and had a nice visit. We left the car with them to use. We caught a jet the next day to go back to our village.

November

This winter we played a lot of pinochle with another couple, it was really fun. I read the Bible at night and crocheted and he played the guitar and sang songs to me.

The lake wasn't frozen over yet and Len made box fish traps out of small boards and baited them inside with salmon eggs. We caught a lot of small trout and they were so good fried crispy. We put some of them in empty Crisco cans. It's cold enough in the outer porch to keep them frozen.

December

The big lake about a mile from our house is frozen over today. Len's uncle loaned us some ice skates and we tried to skate. It was fun until I fell and hit my forehead and it almost knocked me out. My skates were men's and a couple of sizes too big for me, so I had to quit skating. I miss roller skating.

1967
February

We had a very cold, windy winter and the postmaster's wife was having her baby but it was breach and the only midwife here was drunk. They called the Coast Guard but they couldn't come in because the weather was so bad. They got the midwife and poured coffee down her and she was finally sober enough to turn the baby around. We were all so thankful the mother and the baby were okay.

Except for the postmaster, his wife, Ashley and her husband, and the school teacher, the natives in the village drink a lot. They have a barrel of homemade beer brewing all the time. In the summer they would bring whiskey in on the planes and drink straight from the bottle. They would get really drunk. My husband made me go with him when he went to visit his relatives. He started drinking with them again. I felt so bad about it because he hadn't been drunk for quite some time. They were always fighting and mad or crying. They were always trying to get me to drink but I wouldn't. It didn't look like they were having much fun. By God's grace I was never tempted to drink. I would always go into a room away from them and play with the children.

April

We were walking along the beach tonight to go to the village to visit his relatives and play cards. It was cold and windy and the snow from winter was thawing out. It was a very dark night with no moon and we had to use the flashlight.

We were walking along the beach by the bank because the tide was up pretty high. We were walking under an overhanging cliff and all of a sudden we heard big boulders falling all around us. It was really loud and sounded like they were landing a few feet from us. It was a big rock slide and I started screaming and running. We didn't know where to run to because it was so dark you couldn't see where the boulders were falling. We just ran straight ahead as fast as we could. When we got to his relatives' house we told them about it. They said they heard the noise but didn't know what it was from.

After playing cards they gave us a ride home in their skiff. The next day we could see our tracks on the beach and how close the boulders had fallen, only a couple of feet from us.

God was really with us last night, we were so fortunate to not get killed.

May

It's spring and today Mark had been visiting a village quite a distance from ours. When he came back he told us he had gotten married and he had his wife with him. We are so happy for him. She is his first cousin, and she is really nice and comes to visit me and Ashley. It's nice to have another woman to talk to.

Today my sister-in-law's mother moved into what used to be Len's father's small shack. She had been sick and in an institution with tuberculosis, and had a mental problem. I went to visit her and she was drunk. Her little baby is about three months old and has a black eye. I felt so sorry for the baby. I told her daughter about it. She said she would go talk to her about it.

June

This summer the Alaska Packers Company, who owns the cannery, built another big bunkhouse and enlarged the mess hall for everyone to eat in and hired people from California to work in the cannery.

The cannery workers from California are all very friendly to everyone and seem to know a lot about antiques. They went to some of the natives' homes and bought antiques cheaply or for a bottle of whiskey. They bought a very old musket gun from Ashley's husband. They bought a lot of things from Ashley's mother-in-law and father-in-law who were in their 90's.

Len's mother wanted to come and visit us this summer and we said okay. She came in today by plane. It was good for Len to get to visit with her again. She said she had quit drinking. She liked to help with the cooking and we had a nice time together.

She had been with us about a week. When I came home today from visiting the neighbor lady his mother was crying and she was mad. She had packed her little suitcase. I asked her what was wrong and she said Len tried to rape her. I felt really sick to my stomach. He must be really crazy. He hadn't even been drinking today and we had just had some private time together when she was visiting the neighbors. I felt so sorry for her. She cried in my arms and I told her I was sorry.

I took her to the village and she stayed with a relative until she could go home. I was so mad at him. I wanted to leave him but I was so scared of him I didn't say anything to him about it. I was afraid he would beat me. I didn't love him anymore at all and if I just had the money I would leave him right now and never come back to him. I was glad when Len went out fishing with his brother today, they will be gone for a week. I won't have to be around him. I am working in the cannery and was hoping to save enough money to leave him but I have to use it for groceries. I am really enjoying working in the cannery but miss fishing. I like being out on the boat and the water but not with him.

The cannery workers from California brought drugs into the village for the first time. I felt so upset about it. I don't think it will mix very well with the natives' drinking. There are no police here if someone gets out of hand.

A couple of young men that worked in the cannery bought guns and shot some of the animals just for sport which was so sad. The natives were pretty mad about it. We only shoot animals to eat or if we are in danger. I heard someone shot and killed a sea otter and a bald eagle. The eagle washed up on the beach in front of our house. It was so big. I measured the wing span and it was ten feet. I felt so sorry for it. We have no fish and game wardens here to report it to.

When I went to the store today I heard that some young man had also shot and wounded a mother bear that was by the village and killed one of her cubs. It was a grizzly bear, the first one we had seen in this area. We only see Alaska Peninsula Brown Bears and they are really big, some of them 10 feet tall.

This afternoon Ashley and I saw the bear and its cub on the beach not far from our houses. Then she and her cub were on the hill behind the house. Ashley asked me to take her and the children across the bay to the village by skiff. She was going to stay with her mother until her husband came home from fishing. She didn't want to stay home with the bear around because of the children.

I put my dog in the house and I took her and her children by skiff to the village. It was against my better judgment. The wind was blowing hard and the waves were so big. We also had too many people in the skiff. I prayed we would make it, and thank God we did. When I went back home I put a small rope on my dog when he was outside so he wouldn't go after the bear and I kept him inside a lot.

The bear and her cub would sit on the hill by my house and watch me as I was hanging clothes on the clothesline. I had my gun with me hoping I wouldn't have to use it. The mail plane came in and went low over the hill and the mother bear stood up waving her arms around. They came down to the beach and it was fun to watch the baby cub play along the beach with anything he could find. Some cardboard boxes had drifted onto the beach from the cannery and he was playing with them. It was so cute, like a teddy bear. It climbed into my skiff and I discovered later the cub had chewed holes in my gas tank hose. I was lucky I had an extra hose.

I could hear the bear on my outside porch last night. She could smell the salmon I had put out in the porch. Today just before dark I put it outside for her so she won't try to break the door down to get it.

This morning I noticed the salmon was gone as I went to take the clothes off the line. I was just at the corner of the house and had gone about six feet from the house and realized that I had forgotten to take my gun! I started toward the house to go inside to get it. All of a sudden the bear stood up from behind some bushes about six feet away from me. She had the biggest head and teeth and was standing up growling and waving her arms around. She had her cub by her. I was so scared my legs felt like rubber and I could hardly stand up. The only thing I could do to get into the house was to walk right towards and by her very slowly. I thought for sure I was going to be killed by the bear because it was wounded and one of her cubs had been killed and she had one by her. I couldn't believe she didn't attack me. I think there was a guardian angel between the bear and me. I had my back against the house wall and edged my way toward the door on the porch. I made it there without her attacking me. She was still standing up and waving her arms around and showing her teeth and growling at me.

I was able to get inside the house and get my rifle and I came back out. The bear was still in the same place when I came out with the gun. She stood up waving her arms around and growling. I had her in my gun sights, but came to my senses and didn't shoot her. After all, she hadn't hurt me. She ran away with her cub up in the hills.

That night I had a dream that the bear had broken into the house and was standing up at the end of the bed. I woke up with our rifle in my hands pointing it at the end of the bed. It really scared me that I did that in my sleep. We kept the rifle on the wall above the bed. I wasn't going to keep it there anymore! When Len came home from fishing I told him about the bear. He saw her on the beach by the houses. The neighbor man and Len shot at her but she got away, and I was glad.

A young man from California was hired by a fisherman in our village to fish on his skiff. I had heard this from Len but never had met him. Usually the natives just hired natives to be a crew hand on their boats. The young man came in a skiff to our side of the bay in front of our houses out a ways from the beach. I was watching him through the window. He was turning around in sharp circles really fast. He looked like he didn't have much experience with a skiff. He might have been drinking to be doing this. He made a sharp turn in front of Len's uncle's house and the skiff flipped over. I didn't see him come up at all. I can't swim and Len had our skiff at the village.

I ran to Len's uncle's house by ours and he had also seen it happen. I helped him push his skiff out into the water. I really prayed he would be able to find him. He went to where the skiff was and jumped into the water. He kept diving, and was a good swimmer and kept trying to find the young man for some time but couldn't. The water was ice cold he had to give up.

He went to the village to get help. All the fishermen had just come in for the day. They all lined up their boats and hooked their fishing seines together and dragged their nets in the water trying to find him but they never did. It was so sad for a young man to lose his life that way. It was such a terrible thing to happen.

His mother and father came to the village and came to talk to me. They wanted to know about the accident and what happened. I felt so sorry for them and I told them about it. I didn't tell them that I thought a shark or killer whale probably got him. We had seen killer whales in the bay before in a pod and I also saw a huge shark once not too far out from the beach. They didn't stay very long, and I felt so bad for them.

September 5

Ashley's husband found spring water coming from the hillside not too far from our house. The men fixed it so everyone could easily get water from it. It tasted so good!

One of the young men from California that worked in the cannery had been dating one of the native girls here this summer. She was only about fifteen and had never dated before. When he left for California after fishing season she was heartbroken. She thought he would marry her. She took a lot of pain pills and tried to kill herself. I was at the small store in the village today when it happened. The doctor came and got me and had me walk her around in the shower and told me to keep her awake. I had a hard time holding her up and keeping her on her feet. I kept talking to her and she started to come around. She was crying and said he kissed her and told her he loved her and she loved him, and then he left her. Now she had no one. I said God and Jesus loved her and her family and all her friends like me loved her. Her mother heard about her daughter and came and took care of her and I left. I thanked God for letting her live. I felt sorry for her as I knew how much she must be hurting.

September 11

Len's uncle Pete got married to his first cousin today. She had lived with her mother across the bay by the village. She was sixteen and really nice and I enjoyed her company. She visited me often. She wanted to learn how to crochet so I showed her how and she really liked it. She had epilepsy but if she took her medicine she was okay.

September 15

Len was out fall fishing and I was picking berries on the sand spit by myself with my beagle about a half mile from the house. A ground squirrel came out of the rocks. My beagle was so excited and was trying to get it. I threw my jacket over it and carried it home to keep as a pet. I made a nice pen and fed it. In about a month it was eating out of my hand. One day I saw it trying to get out of the pen and felt so sorry for it I took it back to where I found it and let it go. It stayed by my feet and didn't know what to do so I clapped my hands and it ran away and looked back at me as if to thank me and went in the rocks.

September 27

The village got a call today from the hospital in Dillingham informing us that the foxes in our area could have rabies. We had to give shots to all the dogs in the village. I was appointed to do it. I was lucky and didn't get bit. It was kind of frightening since one of the Malamutes Ashley had was mean. I had her hold his head while I gave him the shot. He was only mean because Len's uncle's boy would walk by his kennel where he was tied and throw rocks at him and tease him on his way to school. One day the dog broke free from his rope and bit the boy in the stomach really bad and he almost died. The doctor who came to the village in the summer was still here and was able to save him. They flew him to the hospital that day and he was okay.

October 3

Len's uncle helped him dig for well water today but it came out of the hand pump tasting like salt. We are too close to the beach. They made another outhouse by us and also built a steam bath house. It has an empty oil drum for a stove to put wood in and a big bucket on top of it for heating water. We poured the hot water over rocks stacked around the stove and it would make a lot of steam. It is so nice to take a bath this way.

1968
January

This winter was colder than usual and we had a lot more

snow. We tried to open the door this morning and had to push hard to open it as the snow on the porch was so high. We borrowed a wooden sled from the neighbor. We put a big plastic trash can on it and pulled it to the creek to get water. The creek was all snowed over so we had to listen to find out exactly where the water was running so we would know where to dig through the snow. We had to clear the snow away and chop out steps in the ice to get to the water. I took a small pot and filled it up with water and handed it up to Len to pour into the barrel.

We were almost home with the full barrel of water when the sled hit a soft patch of snow and the sled tipped over and spilled the water. We had to go back and fill up the barrel once more. This time we made it home okay without it spilling. You could walk on top of most of the snow because it had a hard crust but once in a while if you hit a soft spot you would sink in up to the top of your hip boots. It was so cold out the water in the barrel froze on top right away.

I went sledding today on the steep hill behind us. I put my dog on my lap and he really liked it but we tipped over at the bottom. I was afraid the dog would get hurt so the next time instead of using the sled I sat on a big piece of cardboard with the dog on my lap. The snow had an icy crust on it and we really went down fast. It was so much fun!

March

Len ordered a course on automotive body repair. It came in the mail today and he started working on the course. He got bored with it and didn't want to finish it and wanted me to. I didn't want to but he got so mad I finished it for him and passed with a pretty good grade.

April

We saved an eagle from drowning today. It dove in the bay in front of our house for a salt water duck. It had misjudged and went too deep in the water and was drowning. We got in the skiff and used an oar to put under it to keep it from drowning. You could see in its eyes that it was really mad but we were able to keep it afloat and pushed it to the shore and it flew away.

It is spring and we saw a blonde-colored grizzly bear with our binoculars on the cliff across the bay from us. It looked like the same one I had a close call with before and that the men had shot at last summer. She had two cubs with her. She had mated with a brown bear and the little cub was blonde with a wide brown stripe around the middle of it. It was so cute!

June

It's summer and Len's younger sister wrote to us that she had gotten into trouble with the law and would have to go to jail unless we let her stay with us for the summer. We said okay she could come and stay with us. We put a small cot bed in our bedroom against the other wall. She is really nice and I enjoyed her company.

She had been with us about two weeks. She was in the bedroom and Len and I were in the kitchen. He said he wanted to go in and talk to his sister about when they were kids and I should stay out. I heard her screaming and he came out mad and left the house. She said he tried to rape her and that he used to do that when they were kids and she hated him. I am so mad at him I could not believe he would do that to his own sister! I should have known better after trying to do the same thing with his mother. I thought he had changed, but I guess not. I found her a relative to stay with in the village for the summer.

I was too afraid of him to say anything to him about it. I really don't love him at all anymore. He is like two different people. He kisses me all the time and can be so nice and tell me how much he loves me. Then about a year later do things like this and really hurt me. I wish I could make enough money to leave him.

June 7

It is fishing season again and I went to work in the cannery. I doubt it if I will be able to save the $1,500 I will need for airfare to go to Washington and leave him. I hope I can.

I was coming home in my skiff today when a big williwaw (tornado) came across the water right at me. It looked like a big white funnel on the water and I knew I was in trouble. I don't know how to swim and had no life jacket on. I said a prayer and turned the boat around so the wind wouldn't get under the bow and flip me over. It hit me and the skiff hard and the pressure from the williwaw pushed the boat down in the water. If the skiff had gone down just another six inches it would have sunk. It went over the skiff really fast and the boat popped back up again as soon as it went over me. I know it was only because of God's answering my prayer that I didn't sink. I don't know why God is always so good to me and saves me from dying.

September

One of the men in the village, in addition to having a fishing boat, has a crab boat. He makes pretty good money. He bought a movie projector and ordered movies for everyone to watch. You had to pay but it wasn't much. He also had popcorn.

Last night we went and saw "The Birds". It made us laugh because we were around seagulls a lot and we knew that their beaks were not sharp enough to go through wood. When we went home in the skiff it was almost dark and we had to go by an old dock on the way to our house. All the seagulls flew right over our heads, almost hitting us. It was kind of scary after just seeing the movie!

October

Tonight my little Beagle dog didn't come home from hunting. Some days he would be out hunting with the neighbor dogs all day. It was dark out and he always came home by now because he would be tired and hungry. I went outside and called for him but he didn't come so I lit a gas lamp and went looking for him.

I found his tracks on the beach and followed them down towards the sand spit and up to the bank. I called to him and heard him crying. I found him by following his cry. Someone had set four big fox traps and he had all four feet trapped. He was laying there crying in pain. It was so awful to see him like that. He let me undo all the traps even though it hurt him. His little paws were smashed flat. I was crying as I carried him all the way home. I loved my dog so much and I stayed up all night rubbing his feet. My mother always told me if you smashed your finger in a door, keep rubbing it to get the blood flowing and the circulation back.

By morning his paws started looking more normal and I kept working on them that day. In about a week his paws were okay. The neighbor man said it was a good thing I had rubbed his paws or he would have had to have them cut off. He had heard of that happening to someone's dog that had been caught in traps. His uncle didn't trap fox anymore after that.

1969

January

We played a lot of bingo and pinochle this winter. Tonight we were playing bingo at Len's relative's house and the man sitting next to me said you almost have a bingo. Len was so jealous, no man was supposed to talk to me, and he socked the man in the face. It really surprised me because the man wasn't flirting or anything. His aunt got mad and yelled at Len to get out and we left. I was embarrassed and felt so badly about it. He has a terrible temper even when he's not drinking.

February

Len's brother Mark and his uncle Pete got drunk tonight. Mark came to our house and said Pete was mad at him. He said Mark was flirting with his wife so he got his gun. Mark said Pete shoved the gun barrel in his mouth and said he would kill him if he touched his wife. Thank God he didn't pull the trigger. Pete's wife was yelling at him to stop it so he let Mark go home.

Mark came to our house and was telling us about it, and was really mad. Then he went home. After about ten minutes we could hear a rifle being shot and bullets hitting the back wall of our bedroom. Mark wasn't mad at us so we figured he must have been trying to shoot at his uncle's house which was near ours. His shooting was off a lot and he must have been really drunk. I am so glad the bullets didn't come through the wall.

Mark's house is quite a distance from ours. It was pretty frightening.

About three o'clock in the morning, someone was banging on our door. Len was still asleep so I went to the door and Mark's wife was crying and really upset. She asked me to come and help her. She said her husband was drunk and going to shoot her and their little girl with his shotgun. We ran to her house, and when we got inside he was waving his gun around and yelling that he was going to shoot everyone. The little girl was scared and crying. I finally managed to talk him into giving me the gun, without getting shot, and I went back home.

I was glad Len was still sleeping. I didn't want him getting in a fight with Mark.

April 16

Today Mark's mother-in-law was drunk and walking by my house with her little girl who was two years old now. She bent down, opened her mouth and started biting the little girl's arm really hard for no reason. The little girl was screaming. I ran to the woman and made her stop. I brought them inside my house. Her arm was bleeding and I washed it and put some gauze and a bandage on it. I felt so sorry for her. I told her daughter about it and she said she would talk to her mother again.

May 2

A social worker came to the village today from Anchorage. She had been told by someone in the village how Mark's mother-in-law had been abusing her little girl. She went to the couple's shack not far from our place. When she went in they were drunk and giving the little girl whiskey. She took her from the mother and took her to Anchorage to be adopted. I hope she is put in a nice home. It didn't seem to bother the mother at all, but the father who was drunk most of the time was really hurt. He said he missed the girl and said he really loved her and was crying. I couldn't help but feel sorry for him, but I felt sorrier for the little girl when she was with them.

I was walking along the beach by the house today. I heard a baby duck crying by the creek like it was lost. I saw the duck by itself and no mother anywhere. I caught it and took it home. I made a pen by the front porch and fed it. It was really hungry. It was so cute.

Later that day the dog was lying on the porch sleeping by the duck pen and I was inside the house. I heard the baby duck crying and the mother duck answering. I went out on the porch and the mother mallard duck had come after her lost baby and was walking up the path to the pen. I thought what a brave duck she was, and how much she loved her baby to go right by the dog to the pen. I picked up the baby duck and sat it down by her and she walked back down the path with it. They were so happy to be together again.

June

The summer fishing season is here and I went out fishing with Len and Mark. It is opening day of salmon fishing. The whole bay is so full of fish jumping out of the water every couple of feet, it was like a miracle. All the fishermen lined up their boats and when the gun went off everyone set out their nets. Everyone caught and loaded their boats with a lot of fish. A native villager who was 90 years old had never seen or heard of that many fish coming into the bay at once.

Men with fishing boats came from the States this year to fish and everything really changed. They had heard you could make $150,000 in 21 days fishing in our waters. They stole fish from the creeks and put bluestone in the creeks. I never knew what bluestone looked like. I just know it drove the humpback or pink salmon and dog salmon out of the creek into the bay where they could catch them. But when they did this, the fish wouldn't come back to the creek the next year. The fisherman from the lower 48 states didn't care because they didn't live here. It wasn't their only way to make a living like it is for the natives.

Mark said since everyone else was doing it he might as well steal fish from the creek too. Len chased the fish with a plunger out of the creek. I was on the boat. After the fish were in the net and Len was back on the boat, Mark towed the fish in the net away from the creek. He didn't know that when dog salmon hit deep water they dive towards the bottom. There were so many fish, and the pull was so heavy on the net, that it was pulling the snag skiff under water, because one end of the net was attached to the skiff. The seine that was attached to the side of the boat all broke off. Mark yelled to the man in the skiff to jump out. He said he couldn't swim, and he had no life vest on. They kept yelling at him to jump into the water. He did just in time before the skiff was pulled by the fish in the net under the water.

Someone on deck threw him a life jacket attached to a rope and pulled him onto the boat. Of course all of the fish got away and the seine was ripped up and the skiff and motor were lost. We headed home for the day. I don't think they will be stealing from the creeks again.

Today we repaired the seine and got another skiff and motor and we went out fishing again. This the first year the Fish and Game Department came to our village. They started putting their men in the bushes in tents along little bays and creeks. They were trying to catch anyone fishing after hours or illegally. This was very dangerous for the game wardens with so many bears around the creeks.

A Fish and Game agent came out in a rowboat to fine Mark for fishing illegally after hours. Mark yelled at him not to come out to the boat but he kept coming, so Mark shot over the guy's head and he went back to shore. I was so thankful he didn't hit him accidently. That was a crazy thing to do, I couldn't believe he did that!

Today Mark told us a native from another village wanted to start a guide business. He was going to bring men to hunt moose for their antlers. The other natives didn't want this to happen as we had to live off of the moose in the winter months.

When the guide and his customer tried to land their little plane near our village, a native in a three-wheeler shot at the plane and wouldn't let it land. I don't think the guide will try to bring anyone in here again. I don't think the native should have ever shot at the plane. I think he was just trying to scare them and not hit the plane.

Len was out fishing today and I was home. I heard a knock

on the door and to my surprise it was my neighbor from Ferndale, Washington. He was about the same age as my father and his friend. I had known him since I was about eight years old. He was working on a cargo boat that had just come into the bay. I gave him some coffee and visited with him for a while and I asked about my family. He said everyone was okay. It made me really miss them. He told them when he came here he would check on me for them and see if I was okay. He didn't stay long as he had to get right back to the boat.

September

This fall Ashley's husband built a little shack between our houses for his 93 year old father to move into. He had lived by the village, but his wife had passed away recently. He had been living alone until a rockslide fell on his house and buried it. He wasn't in the house at the time thank goodness.

He came down with the flu last week and was really sick. Ashley's husband was out fall fishing and she came over today and asked if I would help her. She thought her father-in-law was dying. I couldn't find a pulse and gave him mouth to mouth resuscitation for but I couldn't save him. He had passed away.

We said a prayer over him and I helped her get him ready for the funeral. We made some flowers out of crepe paper and decorated the church. They buried him on the hill by the church. I really liked him and his wife, they were so kind. It was sad to not have them with us anymore.

1970
January

We have a lot of snow this winter. Today my dog didn't come back home from hunting with the neighbor's big dog, a Retriever. I kept calling for him but he didn't come home. It was getting dark outside and I was really worried about him. He always comes home. I started looking for him. I hiked into the hills calling for him. I was afraid a wolf might kill him. I took the gas lantern and looked for him late into the night. I couldn't sleep worrying about him. Somehow I just felt like he was still alive. There was a lot of deep snow on the ground and

I knew he must be really cold.

I looked for him all day every day. It was the third day and the wind had changed direction. Mark said he heard the dog barking up in the hills. We hiked way up in the hills following the sound of the barking and found him in a deep snow-filled ravine. He couldn't climb up and out of the ravine because the snow was too deep and his legs were so short. The look in his eyes was of pure joy when he saw us.

There was a big wolf at the top of the ravine looking down at the dog. We had gotten there just in time. Len had his rifle with him and shot at it to scare it away. I was so happy to have my dog back. I really loved him. We went down into the ravine and carried him to the top and took him home. He was so glad to be home, he was so cold and hungry.

February

This winter became very cold. The young neighbor children had to walk the two miles along the beach or in the snow every day to school. If the weather was good enough and not too windy, their dad could take them in a skiff but that wasn't very often. He tried to take them in the skiff today and it was so cold there were ice cakes in the water. The skiff's motor broke down and by the time he rowed back to shore the children came very close to having frost bite on their hands.

I was on the village council and they asked me to write a letter to the government to put in a road and airstrip. A lady in the village typed it up for me at the school and we sent it out. It was very dangerous to transport the mail in the skiff the three miles across the bay from where the plane landed on the beach. The wind was always blowing so hard in both summer and winter. The government approved the road and they also would clear the land for a small runway for the mail planes to land. It was such a blessing for the village.

A Canadian shrimp boat came into the bay today and made a haul. Some men went out to the boat to tell them they were not supposed to be fishing in our bay. The Canadians said they would give everyone a lot of the shrimp they caught. They agreed and the shrimpers dumped a big pile of shrimp on the dock for everyone to take home to eat, and then the boat left.

March

Tonight we woke up and the house was so cold inside. The water was frozen in the wash basin. The oil stove went out, it had gotten so cold out that the oil in the drum in the back of the house had turned to jelly and the stove went out. We had to go out in the night in the blizzard with a little propane tank and put the flame on the oil drum to heat it up so we could get out enough oil to put in a five gallon can. We took it inside to fill the carburetor so it started flowing into the stove again. It was so good to be warm again.

With the wind the chill factor was -65 degrees. It was the first time the bay froze over solid. We fed the salt water ducks bread that landed on the ice by the shore to keep them from starving.

June

This summer a man from California came to fish with Len's uncle Bob. Len's aunt and son had left for the summer to visit her Eskimo family up in Northern Alaska. The man fishing with Bob had brought his wife with him. Len's uncle lived about a mile from us on the same side of the bay. He let them stay in his log cabin and he stayed on his boat. This was a big change for Bob's wife. She was very lonesome and would come and visit Ashley and me every day, which we enjoyed.

Today while she was visiting with us, we were outside and saw two bears coming down the hill toward the houses. She asked Ashley if she could use Ashley's .30-6 rifle to try and scare them away. She had never shot a gun before and when she shot it, the kick of the gun made her fall backwards on her hind end. The bears ran away. She was scared of bears and wanted me to stay overnight with her so I did. I left a note for Len in case he came home a day early.

Tonight I woke up and heard Len yelling for me. He sounded mad and I jumped up and grabbed the big flashlight by my bed and ran outside. I heard him swearing and I shined my light towards the sound of his voice and two big bears were a few feet in front of him. They stopped and stood up waving their arms around. When I shined my light on them, they ran away. Len would have shot them but his gun had jammed. Thank God the light shining on them had stopped them from attacking him. Len made a lot of money fishing this season.

Len said Mark received advertising in the mail about wife swapping. Some of the natives started swapping wives from other villages. I heard one man allow three young men to rape his wife, threatening her that if she refused he would beat her. I was thankful Len was jealous, so at least so I didn't have to worry about that. No one made a pass at me, drunk or sober, they were so afraid of him. He had been working out with weights every day for a few years. He was very strong and that was one of the reasons I was so scared of him when he got mad at me. He could lift a 300-pound drum full of oil out of the skiff onto the beach by himself.

August

We went out riding in the skiff today with our dog and came upon several sea otters floating along on their backs. They were eating king crabs they had caught. They put the crab legs on their bellies while floating on their backs and ate them. The dog was trying to get out of the skiff and go after them. We had to stop him because sea otters drown dogs by biting them on the leg and holding them under water. I came across a sea otter at night once when I was walking along the beach on my way home from working at the cannery. It was by some big rocks. I was close to it but didn't see it. I heard a growling noise and it jumped out at me showing its teeth and I ran away from it. They look so cute, you would never think they would be so mean.

Len's cousin came over today to ask me a favor. She was the one who had let me stay with her in Kodiak, until Len sent me money to come home. She asked if I had the keys to Mark's house. I said yes. She said he had made a barrel of beer and invited her husband to come to his house for a drinking party. She didn't drink herself and didn't want him to go to the party. She wanted me to put salt in the barrel to wreck the beer. I said no, I couldn't do that. She got mad and said okay, she would just break a window and go in herself. It was hard to replace windows because they had to be ordered and shipped in, so I said okay, I would open the door but she would have to put the salt in. So she did.

Before the party Mark checked to see if the beer was ready. When he tasted it he got so mad at me. He knew I had a key to his house and thought I must have put the salt in the beer. I told him I was sorry but I didn't tell him about his cousin being in on it. She begged me not to tell on her because her mother would beat her, so I didn't. Mark never did tell Len about it which was nice of him. Mark went to a drinking party in the village instead.

September 6

It is fall fishing season and Mark couldn't go out fishing today. He had a hangover from drinking and felt sick. Len took the boat out and I went with him. Len couldn't get anyone to go out with us. The weather was rough, with big waves and the wind blowing hard.

We came upon a small cove with a lot of fish jumping out of the water so we set the seine out. I was in the snag skiff and circled the fish and brought the end of the net to the boat. Len had to keep steering away from the shore because of the wind so I had to do everything on the deck myself. I had to run the power block and pull in the net and stack leads and corks. I didn't have time to wash the deck off after the last haul and it was slippery with fish slime. I slipped and my chin came down on a bollard, which is a large metal post used to tie up boats. I saw stars and could hardly keep from passing out. I had split the skin on my chin open and it was bleeding a lot but I had to keep working. We managed to catch a lot of fish but it was very difficult and we went home after that haul.

September 7

Today Len went fishing with Mark and his friend and I stayed home. They would be gone for two days. I decided to put more sand from the beach in our five gallon water buckets and bank up around the bottom of the house to keep the cold out. Len had put big two-foot by six-foot planks around the house and pounded stakes in the ground to hold them up. I packed sand for a few hours.

Tonight I heard a clicking noise and wondered what it was. I got the flashlight and could see big sand fleas about an inch long jumping around on the floor. They had come in through a crack where the floor and wall met. I spent a good part of the night killing them and filling the cracks they were coming through with catalog paper.

This morning my right arm really hurts and I can't move it at all, it is frozen stiff. It is really painful and I have no Anacin. I am having a hard time sleeping as the pain never goes away. I read a doctor's book and I think I have bursitis. It is supposed to only last two weeks. It has been a week now and it isn't getting better. I can't eat very much and I throw up because of the pain.

I have lost 10 pounds in a week. Len called a doctor on the shortwave radio. They are sending a small plane today to pick me up and take me to the small town of Dillingham to the hospital. It had been raining a lot and the runway is so muddy the pilot had to carry me to a dry path. He had boots on and the mud was almost up to his knees. We had to go through bushes and they hit my arm and really hurt it.

September 23

The hospital here is small but nice. I am in pain so bad but the doctor is very busy and I can't even have aspirin until he sees me. I have been here for a week now and he hasn't come to see me. The pain isn't quite as bad now and I feel like eating some again. The food is good. I have to go to the lunch room and serve myself from the buffet with one hand as I still can't move my arm at all. They had salmon and moose steaks for us to eat.

The children are in the same hospital as the adults and they run through my room chasing each other throwing comic books at each other and jumping on my bed. I enjoy them being here.

They wanted to know if I would run and slide down the waxed hall floor in my socks with them. I told them no thank you, I didn't feel very good. They are so cute and everyone is so nice to me. I was invited by some 20 year old natives to play poker down the hall but my arm still hurts too much.

Today the doctor came to see me. I have been here two weeks and my arm doesn't hurt anymore and I can move it again. I was released from the hospital today and can go home. I'm so glad to get out of here. They didn't have an empty seat for me on the little Cessna plane so the pilot had me sit on someone's lap.

I flew back home to find out Len had been drinking at his cousin's house. Ashley said her fifteen year old sister came to stay with her overnight. Ashley said Len came home from fishing that evening and saw her sister on the beach and raped her. I felt so sorry for her. He makes me so mad! I told her I was really sorry he did that.

Ashley said they were going to move into a house in the village across the bay because she was afraid Len would rape her girls. I felt so bad about it, I really liked her and the children.

I am so mad at Len! I don't love him anymore at all! I really don't know what to do. I want to leave him, if I only had the money I would. I will miss Ashley and the children so much, we used to visit every day. They are so nice to me. I have to find a way to leave him.

December 12
We received a message from Anchorage today that Len's older sister had died. It was really a shock to us as she hadn't been sick. We felt so bad about it. She was in the car with her husband and children and her husband slapped her hard and it killed her. The police called it an accident and I'm sure he didn't mean to kill her. They seemed to get along well when we visited them the last time we were in Anchorage. Len and Mark won't be able to go to the funeral. The weather is so bad a plane can't come in now.

January

It is a really cold winter and we have had a lot of snow. It is Russian New Year's Eve and most of the people in the village celebrate it because they were part Russian. Len wanted to go to the village to visit Mark and his wife. They were house-sitting for the couple with thirteen children. They had gone to Anchorage for a couple of months. We walked along the beach the two miles to the house where they were staying. Len brought a rifle with us to shoot to celebrate the New Year.

Mark's wife was about five months pregnant. Mark had been drinking and had been beaten up, he looked terrible. Mark said two brothers about sixteen and seventeen years old who lived close by came to visit him. He said the brothers had been drinking too much and smoking pot. They started bragging about how they were the best fishermen and saying things that weren't very nice to Mark. They exchanged words and got in a fight and beat Mark up.

The brothers were gone when we got there. It was dark out. All of a sudden the door was kicked open and one brother had a 45 pistol aimed at Len. The other brother was behind him. I could tell he was going to shoot Len. I tried so hard to reach Len in time to keep him from getting shot.

It was like time stood still and everything was is slow motion. I could see a white wispy cloud go out before me like my spirit went out of my body. Like it was reaching out to him because I wouldn't be able to reach him in time. Somehow I was able to jump in front of him in time. I was looking into the barrel of the 45 pointed at me, I could tell he was going to shoot. Len grabbed the rifle by him and aimed it at the young man with the pistol and was going to shoot him. I pushed the rifle towards the ceiling. The gun went off and made a hole in the ceiling. The young man still had his 45 pointed at me but my sister-in-law was so brave. She grabbed his gun at the same time and shoved it down towards the floor, and it went off. She told me later she could feel the heat of the bullet on her leg but she didn't get shot. The young man ran outside. This all happened in a matter of seconds. Her little boy and girl were only three and four years old and started crying.

About ten minutes later there was a shot from outside. It sounded like a shotgun and it blew the window out. A lot of shooting came from outside into the house. The young man had gotten his young friends he was drinking and smoking pot with. We could hear them yelling and laughing. It sounded like they were all shooting rifles and shotguns and pistols. They started shooting through the windows. I hollered for everyone to get down because there were huge holes in the wall from a shotgun. The holes were going in a circle on the wall all around Mark's head. His wife pulled him down to the floor. The kids ran and got under the bed and everyone stayed down.

Len told me to go upstairs with him. He said he was going to shoot back at them through the window. I yelled at him to tell him not to do that. I had Len's jacket on and was in front of a window. I felt something hot go from the bottom of my foot up my leg. I thought I had been shot from downstairs through the ceiling into my foot. Something made me reach back and touch my bottom and my hand was all bloody. They had shot me through the window in the hind end. That made me so mad!

I knew I was in trouble with no doctor in the village and the weather was so bad a plane couldn't come in. I told Len that I was shot in the hind end and he needed to take me to the postmaster's to radio out for a doctor or a plane to get me to a hospital. He asked if I could walk and I said yes and he helped me downstairs. He was really mad and we went outside and everyone was still shooting, it sounded like a war so many shots were being fired constantly. I could hear bullets hitting everywhere around us.

He was really mad and yelled at them, "You hit someone, are you happy now?" They said yes and kept shooting. My husband yelled at them that he was going to kill them all and I told him that he was not. I was so mad I slapped him in the face and told him he was going to take me to the postmaster's house to get help. It was up the hill about 500 yards away. There was a wood boardwalk but there was too much gunfire to use it.

It was so dark it was hard to see where we were going. The

snow had a hard crust on it and he carried me over his back through the alder bushes. He hadn't gone very far and stepped in a soft spot in the snow and fell and I went down with him. I hit the ground hard right where I had been shot, that really hurt. He quit trying to carry me and drug me through the alder bushes and we stayed as low as we could. We could hear the bullets hitting the bushes around us.

We finally made it to the postmaster's house without getting shot. His wife let us in and let me lay down on a cot with a couple of big towels under me. I kept bleeding from where I was shot and it soaked through two towels before it stopped. I felt weak but by God's grace I wasn't in pain and was glad when it stopped bleeding. Somehow I knew I wasn't going to die and wasn't scared. I knew God was with me and I would be okay.

We could hear the shooting still going on for about an hour. Mark came to the postmaster's house after the shooting stopped and wanted to know how I was. I told him I was okay but I got shot in the hind end. He said he was sorry I got hurt and that they had quit shooting at him, and no one else got shot. Len asked them if it would be okay if he slept by me that night on the floor, they said yes.

The postmaster used his shortwave radio to try and get a plane in the next day but the weather was too bad. If I lay on my back and didn't move I didn't bleed. The first aid lady in the village came to the postmaster's house and put a small bandage on the bullet hole. Her boys were the ones who had started the fight and were shooting at us. I could tell she felt bad. She was a very nice woman.

Today the weather was good enough for a little plane to come in. The hospital in Anchorage where they do surgery was 500 miles away. Len and some other men put me on a stretcher they made and carried me to a skiff, everyone was so nice to me. It was so windy and cold out and they put a blanket over me. The big waves splashed over the side of the skiff and the salt water would freeze right away on the blanket. The skiff pounded so hard because of the big waves, hurting my bottom where I was shot.

They took me across the bay to the beach where a Cessna

plane had landed. He was such a good pilot and he had taken the seats out to get the stretcher in on the floor. There was no room for Len to come with us.

While flying to King Salmon, we hit some kind of air currents that were really bumpy. It was like going over a bumpy road and it really hurt. The pilot said he was sorry it was so bumpy, that he had never been in weather like this before.

When we landed I was taken to a small hospital and put in a waiting room with other people. I was glad I had quit bleeding. After standing in line for a half an hour I saw the clock on the wall and it was 2:30. I knew that a plane wouldn't leave after 3:00 for Anchorage. I needed to be on that plane because they didn't do surgery at this hospital. I said excuse me and I went in front of everyone in line and told the receptionist I needed to catch the plane to Anchorage because I needed surgery. She asked me what was wrong and when I told her I had been shot, she got really upset and asked if I was all right. I said yes. She said she would get the doctor right away.

She put me in a small room and had me lay down on a metal table which was really hard and cold. I was there about thirty minutes and I decided to get up from the table. It was really hard and uncomfortable. I lost my balance and started to fall. The doctor had just come in and caught me. He wanted to know if I was okay. I said yes, and he said good because he was delivering babies and had two more to deliver and he was the only doctor there. Then a nurse came and took me to a bed and said it was really cold out, thirty below. The small army jet I would take to Anchorage couldn't take off until the weather warmed up. She gave me an aspirin but I wasn't in pain. I was so thankful to God that I wasn't in pain.

Today it had warmed up enough at noon that the plane could take off. I was put on a stretcher in the aisle with a plane load of young service men. I could hear them asking each other what had happened to me. Someone said she got shot in the butt. Some of them started laughing. It didn't bother me as they were all so young and didn't mean anything bad by laughing. It was a kind of funny place to get shot. The two older men in charge of me didn't like it and told them to knock it off.

In Anchorage I was taken in an ambulance to the hospital. It was really cold and they covered me with a lot of blankets. The two young men in the ambulance were so kind to me. They didn't operate on me that night because the five doctors were discussing with each other about whether to operate or leave the bullet in me. I wanted it out because I could feel it there and it hurt.

In the meantime a police officer came and questioned me about what had happened. I was almost finished telling him what happened and I started to not feel so good for the first time. I knew I was going into shock. The doctors made him leave and they gave me a shot of something to put me to sleep.

The next day the head doctor went against the other four doctors who wanted to leave the bullet in and said he was going to operate. He was worried that some of the fabric of the clothes I had been wearing could have been brought into the wound by the bullet and could cause an infection. He had been a doctor in the service and operated on a lot of men in Vietnam and said it was always better to remove the bullet. He was right because the material was still there and had caused a bad infection. I had gangrene from the four days with the bullet in me and a high fever. The doctor told me I might lose my leg from the knee down. I told him I didn't care, at least I was alive.

I was in surgery eight hours. When I woke up from surgery I was really hungry and they gave me some moose steaks. It was so good! I thanked God for letting me live. The doctor said the bullet had gone in my right buttock and had nicked the biggest nerve to my leg quite a bit. It had made a hole in my pelvic bone and cracked it. The doctor said if it was a certain kind of staph infection in the bone he wouldn't have been able to stop it.

I was on the critical list and was hooked up to antibiotics for a week. I was so hot from fever. I didn't call my mother because I didn't want to worry her and she didn't have money to come and see me anyway.

On the third day, I got tired of being in bed and got up and pushed my stand with the bags of antibiotics with me up and down the hall, but someone told me I was bleeding so I had to go lay down. Towards the end of the day my antibiotics ran out. I knew they were short of doctors and nurses so I rang my buzzer and asked them where they kept them. They showed me where they were and how to hook them up so I could get them myself from then on.

Art Len's brother who was still in the Navy and on leave had been visiting his younger sister, came to see me. He was so nice to come and visit every day. I had so many visitors the next week. All of Len's relatives who lived in Anchorage just for the winter but had houses in our village came to see me. They wanted to know what happened. They said they heard the big old two story house was really shot up with bullet holes every few inches. They were so nice to me but I got too tired talking to everyone for hours every day and didn't feel very well so the doctor had them leave.

I heard Len was coming today. I have been here a week now. The nurse had fixed my waist long hair nice for me. I was looking forward to seeing him. When he came I could tell he really didn't care about what had happened to me and didn't want to stay and visit. That really made me realize he didn't love me at all. He said he couldn't get a plane to come sooner. After being with me about a half hour he left and went out in the hall. He either didn't know I could see him or didn't care. He was in a phone booth with a young native girl kissing her. He didn't come to see me anymore after that.

A couple of days later Len's sister, who had stayed with us one summer, came to see me. She wanted to know if I would like to come and stay with her at her apartment until I got well. I said yes, my fever was gone and I felt better. I really wanted out of the hospital. I had been there for 10 days. I asked the doctor and he said okay only because she lived close to the hospital and she said she would change the bandages for me. The doctor said I would have to keep coming back to the hospital every couple of days so he could check my wound. He said I should really be in the hospital for two months, not just ten days.

The doctor said he had to pull out the drainage tube he had put in my buttock down to my pelvic bone. He said it would hurt and to hang onto the bed railing. I had no idea it would hurt so bad. I heard someone screaming and it was me. It quit hurting so much when it was out.

Len's sister took good care of me. I was tired and slept a lot. I had to sleep on my sides and couldn't sit. The doctor said the best place to get shot is the butt because of all the padding. I started getting sharp pains and would sometimes scream it would be so unexpected like a knife stabbing me. It was because of the nerve in my leg that was hit. It was a miracle from God that I didn't have a limp and could walk okay.

Of course I never saw my husband during the two weeks I stayed with his sister. I really didn't care anymore. I guess he was having fun with his new girlfriend. He finally came one day and said he had plane fare, that the Bureau of Indian Affairs (B.I.A.) was flying us home. I thanked his sister for letting me stay with her and went home with him even though I really hated to. I couldn't stay there as she only had one bedroom and I was sleeping on the sofa. I wish I had the money to go to my parents in Washington.

February

Today he told me that he really wanted to move back to Anchorage. He couldn't sleep at night. He was afraid because of the shooting and always thought he heard noises outside at night and couldn't sleep. He was constantly making plans on how to kill the people who had shot at us.

We had to go to the village today to get supplies and I stayed by the skiff by myself while Len went to the store. The two brothers who had shot at us landed on the beach in their skiff right by me. One made a comment, making fun of me getting shot in the butt, but his brother came and told me he was sorry he shot me. He said he thought it was Len because I had his jacket on. I told him it was okay, I knew he didn't mean to. He was actually a nice kid, he was just drunk and on pot for the first time. He was a really good artist and he could paint beautiful pictures freehand of landscapes and animals. He had an amazing talent.

March

Len sold the house for $900 and sold our skiff and outboard motor. We flew to Anchorage and took our dog with us. I would rather live with him there than here. Maybe I can get a job and make enough money to leave him. When we got out of the plane it was forty below and was like stepping into a freezer. Our eyelashes froze up right away. We went to the Bureau of Indian Affairs office and told them why we had moved here. They set us up with a small single-wide 12-foot trailer, and an old car. They gave us $1,000 cash and food stamps. They got him a job working for the city in the sewer system. He would come home with really old coins. He bought a coin book but none were in mint condition and not worth anything. We had our little Beagle with us, and he didn't like to go outside much because of the cold.

The B.I.A. offered me a job as a file clerk helping with the Alaska Land Claims Act. They said I would have to get my GED. first. I hadn't graduated high school because of getting married but always had good grades in school. I had taken a business course in high school. I took the car tonight to go take the GED test and passed it. I went to the car and there was a blizzard outside. One hour ago when I went inside it wasn't even snowing. I had never driven in snow before and there were cars along the side of the road in the ditch. I drove real slow and made it home okay.

I got the job working for the B.I.A. I was amazed that quite a few of the families who summited an application had sixteen children.

The man I was working for was supposed to be checking thousands of applications that were sent to the office by natives. They had to be one quarter native, so they could qualify to claim land. There were so many applications he could never check them all in time for the deadline. There were stacks and stacks of papers. He would just hand them to me unchecked and tell me to file them. It was overwhelming as there were not enough workers. Len didn't want me working there, he was jealous of the man I was working for. I told him I wasn't going to quit working. I really liked working there and making some money.

March 19

Today it was so cold that the oil in the oil tank outside of our trailer turned to the consistency of jelly. We had no heat and thousands of other people didn't have any either. We had to take a blow torch to the tank to unthaw it. We had to run a cord from the trailer to the car and have a heater under the hood of the car.

We saved money and rented a small house that was bigger and nicer than the trailer and it was furnished. The owner was a Japanese lady and she was very nice to us. She invited me to her house for lunch and gave me dried seaweed and some brine shrimp that was really salty. I had a hard time not throwing up.

Len went to a lawyer and tried to sue the young men who shot me. The lawyer said he would never get anything. He said if we were in the lower forty-eight states we would get a million dollars but not in Alaska. I didn't want to sue them anyway. Len and I got a call from the state attorney we were assigned to. We had to go tell him the story about the shooting. Len had to go to court in Kodiak but I couldn't be at the trial or testify because it was a shooting and therefore a crime against the state and they take over. Len said most of the jury looked like homeless people and were on drugs and laughed when they heard where I got shot. He got really mad about that.

The father of the two young men that shot me said his boys would never go to jail. He had a lot of money because he had a big crab boat and a fishing boat. The sheriff that came to our village testified he had never seen a big old two story house so full of bullet holes. Not a foot was left that didn't have holes in it. The young men were sent to a camp in Anchorage for two weeks. They said they played pool and had a good time there and they laughed about it. The Sheriff said the jails in Anchorage were full and sent them back to the village. Their father lied and told the sheriff I was drunk. Some of the people in the village were mad about that because they all knew I never drank alcohol. I didn't care because I didn't want them to go to jail anyway.

The weather here is so different than in our village. Spring comes earlier in the year in April and the summer is much hotter. It is June and I cannot believe it is 100 degrees outside. It is a real dry heat. It is so nice to not have rain all the time and for it to be so nice and warm out.

I am still working at the B.I.A. and Len is still working for the city. He has been so nice to me and hasn't been drinking. We visit friends and play bingo at a bingo hall in the evenings. We went to the county fair this weekend and they let us take the dog as long as he was on a leash. The dog had never seen a cow before and was really scared of them. That night he had nightmares and was growling and crying in his sleep.

The vegetables from Palmer are really big. They grow 30 pound cabbages, they were huge. We had fun, it had been a long time since I had been to a fair.

December 10

It is December and Christmas and I put up a small tree. It was nice to decorate for Christmas again. This was the first time that we put up a tree since we were married, as there were no trees in our village. We went grocery shopping and there were two reindeer tied to the parking meters in front of the store for people to see. They seemed tame but I felt sorry for them.

December 12

We went to our friend's house tonight. He was the baker who came to our village with his Eskimo wife in the summer to work for Alaska Packers. The men were playing cards and the women were visiting in the kitchen. They were all Eskimos and were slicing frozen moose meat thin and eating it and whale blubber raw. They wanted me to eat some but I just couldn't bring myself to eat raw meat. I always like my steaks well done. I did try a little piece of the frozen sliced whale blubber but I didn't like it. When we left to go home there was a moose lying down resting by the front steps. Someone had put a hat on his rack, he was really tame, so cute!

Len and I were able to get the same vacation time off. My parents were living in Seattle now and we flew there to visit them for two weeks. We took our dog with us. It was so good to see my family again. I had written my mom a letter about the shooting in the village while I was in Anchorage. I hadn't told her anything about Len being unfaithful and mean to me in my marriage. He was being so nice to me for a year now. I just wanted to have a nice visit with them.

The next day all of my brothers and sisters came to visit us. My mother and I had prepared a big meal at her house and everybody brought something to eat. We had all been visiting and were just sitting down to eat when my sister, who Len liked, was kidding with him. She said he would look good with a crew cut, which was the style now. He got so mad he jumped up from his chair and told me we were leaving. I said no, I wanted to stay and visit my family. I said he could go if he wanted to. He was really mad and grabbed my arm and pulled me out the door. I tried to get away from him but couldn't. I saw the surprised look on everybody's face, the men got up and didn't like what he was doing. I didn't want the men in the family to get in a fight with him. I was so scared of him but went with him.

He rented an apartment and made me stay there with him

and wouldn't let my family come to see me and wouldn't let me go to see them.

For two weeks he just wanted to stay inside the apartment and watch T.V. He let me talk to my family on the phone but he would listen and didn't like me to talk very long or he would make me hang up. It was like he was jealous of them.

I was walking my little dog today and as we went by a house a Poodle came out to fight my dog. I picked my dog up and the Poodle bit me hard on the leg. It really hurt. The lady came running out and said she was sorry and that the dog was old and blind. She said the dog had its rabies shots. She was really sorry and I told her I was okay. It was deep but I didn't need stitches.

December 21

He wants to go back to Anchorage and not stay here another week. I wish so bad I could stay and be with my parents for Christmas.

I dread going back to Anchorage with him. I was hoping to get away from him, but he didn't let me out of his sight. I said a sad goodbye to my family on the phone and we left Seattle and flew to Anchorage today.

The pilot was trying to land at the Anchorage airport but a blizzard had come in fast with some big williwaws going across the runway. The pilot came on the loud speaker and said we had a problem. He said it would be really hard for him to land because of the strong winds (williwaws) but he didn't have enough gas to make it back to any other city.

We could see the white wind funnels whipping across the airstrip and the jet plane was being bounced around. I think everyone in the plane was scared and praying and I know I was. The pilot tried to land three times and had to pull up each time. He came on the loud speaker again and said he had to land now as we were almost out of gas. The wind hit us hard and I was sitting by the window over the wing and looked out the window. I could see the wing of the plane tipping way over to the side nearly hitting the pavement. The plane straightened out and we landed. Everyone was cheering and I thanked God for letting us land safely.

1972
January

Len's cousin Kyle came to Anchorage and they started going out together to bars at night and not coming home all night. The next day when I took the car to go get groceries I found a woman's purse on the car seat. It really upset me as Len had been faithful to me for a year or more and I thought he had changed. I was going to find a way to leave him!

When he got home he wanted to make love to me, but for the first time I told him no. He slapped me hard and he left in the car. That night I called his cousin Kyle and asked if he knew where Len was. He said Len had been seeing a prostitute. He must have taken her purse to her. He didn't come home tonight I was glad.

I called the lady we rented from, she and her husband were so nice. I told her I was leaving Len and why. She said I could stay in her spare bedroom. I told her I would pay her rent until I could get an apartment to rent. I moved in with them tonight. I had very few clothes or belongings to pack. I hated to leave my dog but I knew Len would take good care of him.

My job at the B.I.A. ended so I started looking for a job and tried to join the Navy. They said I was too old as I had just turned 30 last July. I tried the police department but when I applied they asked me if I had ever been in a shooting. I said yes, but it wasn't my fault. I never shot anyone. I just got shot trying to keep everyone from shooting each other. They said they couldn't hire me. I was really disappointed as I was in really good shape and a good shot with a rifle and 45 pistol.

I started calling everyone in the phone book looking for a job and got hired at a dental lab as a trainee. I really liked the job and made good money, about $600.00 a month and they liked my work. I answered the phone and took messages and learned how to make dentures and delivered teeth to dental offices. I had just enough money to pay the Japanese lady her rent and get food but not enough to save up any money. The food was so expensive here.

I was the only one at the office when Len came to my job. I was so scared when I saw him, he looked so mad. He said he wanted me to come back with him to the village to go fishing in June. I said no. He grabbed me and started pulling me out of the office. I was screaming and tried to get away but couldn't. He shoved me in the car and said he would change and be faithful to me. I didn't believe him but I had go with him, I was so scared he would beat me up. He never let me out of his sight.

I called the Japanese lady and she brought my things to the house that Len was still renting from her. I was so mad at her and asked her why she had told him where I was working. She said Len came to her house crying and saying how he wanted me back. She had promised me she wouldn't let him know where I was. She either felt sorry for him or it was because she had told me her son was coming from Japan to live with them. Maybe that was why she told him where I worked, maybe she needed the bedroom.

My dog was so glad to see me, I had missed him a lot. I called my job and explained to them that I had to leave town and said I was sorry. I had really loved my job. We sold our car to a dealer who asked me a couple of questions I had to answer. I could tell Len was really mad because I had talked to him. We took a plane back to the village that day.

We had sold our house and didn't have a place to stay. One of Len's relatives had moved to a house closer to the cannery. They let us stay in their empty house across the bay from where we had lived. It was about a mile from the cannery.

When we got into the house he grabbed me by my long hair and threw me on the bed. He made a fist like he was going to hit me. Then he started choking me and let go just before I passed out. He said he didn't like me talking to the car dealer. I wish I would have found some way to escape from him. I have lost all hope of him ever changing.

Today I was washing the walls and there were sewing needles sticking into the wall instead of a pin cushion. I didn't see them and when I came down with the washrag I hit a needle and it went clear into my thumb so you couldn't even see it anymore. We called the doctor through the shortwave radio but they said to just leave it there and it would be okay, that my skin would make a cocoon around it.

I started to get a big bump on my wrist and it really hurt so I went to the doctor in Dillingham. He didn't have anything to give me for pain but gave me something to bite down on as he dug deep into my thumb. I didn't want to scream because he had his little six year old boy with him and he was watching. I didn't want to scare him. He didn't want to lance it and he got it out, but it really hurt.

I flew home in a small Cessna plane. The weather got so bad with the snow causing poor visibility and the wind making the little plane bounce around. We couldn't make it to our village and we had to land in a village about twenty miles away. There was no landing strip and we had to land on the ice on the lake. The pilot was new to the area and so was I. We could see some natives waving to us at the edge of the ice and we thought they were waving for us to land by them. We landed and I got out. I could hear them yelling at us not to land because the ice was too thin.

The pilot took off again right away. They couldn't believe the ice had actually held us and that we didn't sink. I think it was because God was really with me again today. I was so thankful to Him. He was always there for me, saving me from dying.

A young couple took me in their skiff twelve miles to our village. I went to the house we were staying in. Len wasn't home and I went to find him to tell him I was back. I went to the first house by us where his aunt lived. The men and Len were drinking and playing cards in the kitchen. They didn't see me. His aunt that was married to one of the men at the table was passed out from drinking and lying on the bed naked. I covered her up and went back home. I felt sorry for her that they took advantage of her when she was drunk.

I was sitting on the cliff by the house, looking out over the village and asked God when he was going to get me out of this hell hole. That night Len came home and I was doing dishes and Len was lying in bed. He suddenly jumped up and put his hands around my throat and started choking me. I almost passed out but I was fighting him and he let me go. I was so scared and asked him why he did that. He said he was just lying there thinking about what he would do to me if I ever looked at another man. He really must be crazy. He left fingerprint bruises on my neck. I had difficulty breathing while laying down at night after that. I had to keep swallowing often or I would choke. I have to get away from him before he kills me.

April

Today we went duck hunting and when we returned Len's 12 year old cousin Ricky came to visit us. Ricky picked up the shotgun and pulled the trigger. I think he must have been drinking to have done that. The buckshot went right by my head. I had my back to him and could actually hear the buckshot go by my ear. It made a big hole in the wall. It was a miracle from God that I wasn't hit.

I was so scared! I know he didn't do it on purpose and he was really sorry. Len was really mad at him.

June

Len went out fishing with Mark and I worked in the cannery making cans again. It was fun getting to visit with the women again, they are so nice to me. Today during break we were throwing folded up cotton work gloves at each other. I threw one at my friend and she ducked and it hit the mechanic who had just come in. Len must have gotten back from fishing early and he walked by and saw me and thought I had thrown it at the mechanic. He looked really mad. I was afraid to go home. We had to work late tonight and I was hoping he would be sleeping. He was awake when I got home and was mad. I explained to him what had happened and he calmed down.

Len's brother Art, who had served three years in the Navy by then, came home to the village. He was so nice and everyone really liked him and was glad he was home. Ashley's brother Chet hired Art to fish with him this summer. Art went out fishing today with Chet and the rest of the crew. In the afternoon they started drinking and they all got drunk, even Chet, who was the captain of the boat.

The weather got really bad and the wind came up and the waves were huge. Art fell off the boat. They tried to rescue him but because they were drunk and the water was so rough it took a while to get him aboard the boat. They tried to save him, but couldn't and he died.

It was a real shock to everyone and very hard on all of us. I really liked Art, he had been so nice to visit me every day in the hospital. Chet was a really nice person and he felt so bad about it. Because he was the captain and was drunk, he blamed himself.

Art was buried in the cemetery by his brother and father on the hill looking over the bay. They held a service in the Russian Orthodox Church and a priest came in to oversee the funeral.

September

After fall fishing a strong wind came in really fast. Len's uncle had a wind gauge that clocked the wind at 120 mph.

We went outside to see if we could walk against it. We had to get real low to the ground to walk against it but it would push us backward if we stood up. We decided it was too dangerous because a piece of wood or something could hit us, so we went back inside. We had put a thick wood stick in the front of our Plexiglas bay window for a brace so the window wouldn't break. The next day the wind was back to normal, which was almost always 35-50 mph.

Today we walked over to the village to talk to everyone about the wind. A terrible thing had happened. Last night Ashley's brother Chet and another young man had gotten drunk. Chet had recently married a girl in another village about 12 miles away and wanted to go home to her. The men were so drunk they didn't realize how strong the wind was, it was hurricane strength. As they went down the dock to get in their skiff, Chet's 12 year old brother tried to stop them but he couldn't and they shoved him away. He ran home and got some men to follow him back to stop them but it was too late. Chet and his friend had already left the dock in the little skiff.

It was dark and the dock lights were on but they couldn't see the young men anywhere in the skiff. Everyone was drunk and nobody wanted to go out in the hurricane. They knew they would never survive out there and that the two men had probably already drowned in the huge waves.

The two men were never found. It was so sad. His wife kept searching the beach for miles for two weeks. A lot of the men went in fishing boats to look for them or any kind of skiff wreckage. One native man had an airplane and searched but never found them or any wreckage. His mother had me take her out in the middle of the bay and she threw a wreath of paper flowers she had made for him into the water. We said a prayer for him. I felt so sorry for her.

1973
January 28

It is winter and really cold, about ten below zero. Len and I went down the beach about a half mile to the old house his cousin Kyle and aunt used to live in. It had been halfway blown down by the twisters and the recent hurricane. The waves had washed some of it away. We will go there every day this winter and work on tearing it down. Len will tear down the wood walls on the house and I will straighten out the nails with a hammer and use them on the house we are going to build. There are no nails in the store here. It is very cold out, but because we get so warm from working hard we have to take our jackets off.

We have been working for two weeks now. We are going to tow the wood by skiff to an area about twelve miles away. We are going to clear a plot of land and build a house. The land has a waterfall on it and the water tastes so good from it! The house will be about twenty yards from the beach.

February 16

We finished tearing down the house today and stacking up the wood to be towed to the plot of land we have. Len hasn't been drinking and is being so good to me. He has changed a lot. He tells me how much he loves me, and is so loving and kind.

May

This spring Alaska Packers loaned Len the money to buy a skiff and an outboard motor, a seine and a small power block. He also bought a really big skiff. He mounted a small power block in the big skiff. We will use it with the snag skiff so we can fish like the big fishing boats. We also will have the advantage of going into shallow water to get the fish where other boats can't go until the tide comes in.

June

Fishing season started and we are doing really well. Alaska Packers is giving the fishermen better prices for the fish now. They are trying to compete with the freezer boats that are coming into the bay. The men who own their own boats can sell to them and get really good prices. Mark came to Len tonight and wanted Len to deliver some fish for him to the freezer boat because he got so much more money from them. He took them from his boat and put them in Len's skiff. He didn't want Alaska Packers to know or he would lose his lease for their boat. Len delivered the fish and Mark gave him $600.00.

We made $4,000 in about 15 minutes in one haul and about $20,000 this summer in twenty-one days.

September

We went fall fishing with Mark and made some more money. We took our dog with us fishing today and he helps me spot fish jumping out of the water. He barks when he sees one and I know there are a lot of fish where he is looking. It was fun. We helped clean the boat up and put it away for the year.

Today we went hunting with Mark and got a moose. Next week we will go up the river with him and get some salmon to smoke and freeze.

October

We wrote to the Bureau of Land Management and filled out papers for homesteading. We went to the place where our cabin was going to be built today. We started clearing the land just enough to build a cabin, a shed, and a smokehouse. The whole area was full of salmonberry bushes which are similar to raspberry bushes. The roots are really hard to dig up. We did a lot of digging and chopping with an axe and hatchet to get the bushes and roots out. It was a lot of work. I got stung by a big bumblebee under my arm and it almost made me pass out. I put some mud on it and it got better. We also dug a huge hole for a septic tank so we could have a toilet.

Len's dad had been a carpenter at one time and taught Len how to build a cabin. He drew up his own blueprints for the cabin. We towed the wood with our skiff in the water from the old house we had torn down. It was about 12 miles to where we were going to build our cabin. We have to get it built in two months before it starts raining and snowing and the ground freezes. We had to build it by hand because we didn't have electricity.

Len sawed all the wood boards and I nailed the wood on the walls and floor. The floor was tongue and groove wood. He was helping me nail the walls, and got mad for no reason. He is changing and his temper is back again when he works on the house. He threw the hammer at me and almost hit me and called me stupid. I don't know why he gets so mad. He is always swearing, saying the F word, maybe he is tired. He really scares me sometimes.

We put heavy 2x12 planks on the roof and heavy corrugated tin on top of that and nailed it down with spikes because of the wind called williwaws.

I had taught my dog how to climb up a ladder. I was up on the roof working and was surprised when I turned around to see my dog on the roof coming to be with me. It was slanted but not real steep. I had to help him back down the ladder. We just got the roof on and had almost finished the cabin before the winter came except for the fixtures inside. We put in a big bay window made out of Plexiglas so the bears couldn't break in.

This cabin is by the ocean, only about 20 yards from the surf. The waterfall was only about a hundred yards from the house. There was also a reef and big boulders about 20 yards out from the beach by our house. You have to raise your voice to talk above the steady loud noise of waves crashing against the rocks, pounding surf and the waterfall noise. Our other house was in a bay protected by a big sand spit.

We ordered bathroom fixtures and a kitchen sink and a small generator so we could have a light at night. We also ordered a bed, mattress, and bed springs. Whenever the weather permitted we came and worked on the house all winter.

1974
June

It is spring and we had finished the cabin and moved in. I really like our new cabin. I noticed a magpie on the beach today and decided to tame it. I put some salmon on the beach and stood still, not far from the salmon, and the magpie would come and take it away. Each day I would put it closer to me and sit real still. In about three weeks the magpie was eating out of my hand. It had babies and she brought all five of them to me to feed. They followed me everywhere and would sit on the porch railing and cry for food at 4:30 in the morning. I didn't like getting up that early in the morning but I did anyway and gave them some fish to eat. They were really cute.

Len has really changed and is being so nice to me. Today we went fishing not far from our cabin. We were fishing for halibut with a hand line made of heavy twine with a big heavy 3 inch hook on the end. We baited the hooks with big pieces of fresh salmon. We tied the end of the line to the skiff and threw the rest overboard. We hooked something so big it started towing the skiff so we cut the line. There were humpback whales where we were fishing and one might have swallowed our bait.

Later we caught a really big halibut and it put up such a fight we had to shoot it in the head with a pistol and use a gaff hook to try to get it in the boat. The wind was blowing so hard and rocking the skiff that we had a hard time getting it in the boat. I was able to grab a hold of it and help pull it in. We cleaned it and weighed it and it was 220 pounds, with the insides out of it.

Today we went out halibut fishing again and set out a skate. It is a rope with corks on it and weighted lines going down with baited hooks with salmon on them. We caught four halibut all over a hundred pounds in about three hours. We were re-baiting the hooks with salmon when a big killer whale came up out of the water right by the boat rocking it and almost tipped the boat over! We headed for shore fast. That was really scary! We were thankful to get back to the beach. We used octopus for bait after that, and it will be harder for the king crab to take the bait off the hooks. We gave some halibut to Len's relatives in the villages. The halibut was so good fried, and we dried some also.

Today we waited five hours before we checked the skate and all that was left of the halibut were the heads full of huge sand fleas. When we pulled the skate in the bottom of the skiff was full of the big sand fleas. They were so awful looking. We had to clean the skiff out when we got home. We will check the skate sooner next time.

The fishermen all heard about the halibut and will be setting up their boats to fish for halibut after the salmon fishing season.

June 5

We were in our skiff today going 12 miles to the village from our new house to get groceries. The shaft on the outboard motor broke. Another storm had come up fast and we were being swept out into the ocean by a very strong wind and tide. We were three miles from the village and were being blown behind a sand spit where no one would be able to see us from the village. The waves not too far from us were so huge we would sink after the first one hit us. We threw out the anchor but it couldn't touch the bottom and grab hold in the sand, the water was too deep. I put my parka, that had orange on the inside, on the end of an oar and waved it but it seemed hopeless. I started praying really hard. Len rowed so hard against the wind, tide and big waves, the oak oar broke in half. He couldn't reach shore, only about 20 feet from us.

The wind kept pushing us back towards the huge waves. We had a rifle and he fired it three times and then again three times. A man from the States had just come to the village to fish for the summer. He was on the cannery dock and recognized the shots as a distress signal. We saw a skiff coming towards us. We waved and I prayed he would get to us in time. He came to us and threw us a line. He towed us away just before we came to the big waves. We got to the village okay and fixed the motor. Had the people living in the village heard the shots we fired they would have just thought it was someone out hunting.

I believe God heard my prayer and sent a guardian angel to save us. I couldn't sleep that night and felt inspired to write a poem, so I did, thanking God for saving us. I always liked to write poems.

June 7

Today we saw a humpback whale go by our cabin and we got in the skiff and ran along side of it. It came up out of the water really close by us and the barnacles on its back smelled bad. I was scared we were going to be tipped over, but it reached a deep channel and we didn't see it anymore.

This afternoon I was looking out the window and saw two big Alaska brown bears fighting on the sand spit across from our cabin not too far away. I watched them with the binoculars and they were standing up fighting each other, they were really quick. You could hear them growling, and one chased the other away.

June 12

The oil company found oil right by the river that the fish went upriver in to spawn. The natives wouldn't let them drill because it would ruin the fishing. We were looking out our window today and we heard a helicopter from the oil company go over. When it got low over the sand spit it hit an air pocket, and crashed on the ground but didn't catch on fire. We jumped in the skiff and went to the helicopter. Thank God they were okay and were walking away from the helicopter. They were pretty shaken up but not hurt. We gave them a ride to the village, where they could get help.

June 16

My dog saw a muskrat today in the water in front of our house and went in after it. I called to him but he wouldn't come back. I was in my hip boots and went in after him. The water came up over the top of my hip boots and was really cold but I didn't care if I got wet. I knew the muskrat would drown my dog. I grabbed him by the collar and pulled him out of the water. The muskrat had hold of his foot biting it but it let go when it saw me. Len shot the muskrat because he was afraid it would drown the dog some other time. My dog's foot was bleeding but not broken.

June 20

It is fishing season again. We were sitting in our cabin by the kitchen window and saw salmon in the ocean jumping out of the water. They were right in front of our house. It was a big school of fish. We got in our 18 foot boat that he had put a small seine in and had installed a small power block. We made a haul, and caught a lot of fish. All the red salmon went by our house from the ocean and up a river to spawn. The magpies followed me out fishing today and would sit on my skiff and want me to give them some salmon.

July

Len and I went out fishing again today and we saw some salmon jumping a lot in one area. The tide was pretty low and the other boats couldn't get to them but we could as we could go in more shallow water. We made a haul and caught a lot of fish. We could hold 800 salmon in the skiff I was in. Len could put some in his. We delivered them and went back for more. A couple of boats were not too happy about it and were trying hard to get into the area but couldn't until the tide was higher.

We were leaving with our skiff full of fish and we got stuck. Len wanted me to jump out and push the boat but it looked like it would be over my head and I can't swim. I didn't want to, I was scared, but he got so mad I did. The water came up to my shoulders and I was able to push enough to get us going again. He gets so mad sometimes.

It is so hard to fish in the lagoon anymore. For some reason that no one knows, the lagoon is full of green algae this year. It clings to the net and fills it full and is hard to save the fish and to pull it in because it is so heavy. We made a lot of money fishing this season. The summer season is almost over, only a couple of weeks left.

Today it is very windy and stormy out. Len needed some parts to fix the outboard motor and a 50 gallon drum of oil for the oil stove. He told me about 3 o'clock to go to the store in the skiff and get the parts and the oil for him.

The store was about five miles from us. I told him it was really bad weather as the wind was blowing about 40 mph. I asked if I could go tomorrow when the weather was better. He got so mad and said he needed the parts now! I was so scared of him that I went and prayed to God to keep me safe. I knew it would be really dangerous coming back in rough seas with a drum full of oil in a small skiff. The skiff would be really low in the water. I got to the store okay.

The store manager was really upset that Len sent me for the parts and oil in bad weather. He was worried about me getting back okay. I had a really hard time getting back without sinking, the waves were so big. They were coming over the sides of the skiff but I had a big five gallon bucket to bail with while running the skiff. I started praying. I was glad I had been in rough weather before when fishing and running the snag skiff. I had to go in and out of the huge waves and try to miss the big ones so I wouldn't sink. I finally got back and thanked God for letting me get home okay.

Instead of Len being glad to see me like I thought he would be, he was really mad at me. He said I was stupid and was yelling at me that I got the wrong parts. I showed him the list he gave me to give to the manager. He had checked them all off and they were all the right parts.

He just got madder and went into the bedroom and lay down. I was sitting at the kitchen table and he was calling me all kinds of names. He said he didn't love me anymore and was getting madder by the minute and yelling louder and louder. Somehow he was different, really out of control and sounded weird. He got so worked up I started shaking in my chair. I knew he was going to come into the kitchen and kill me but I didn't know why. It wasn't that long ago he was saying how much he loved me.

Then I realized why he was so mad. He had been hoping I would drown in the boat and die. I got up from my chair as quietly as I could and went out the door. It was getting dark out but the moon was out just enough to see where I was going. I would walk the twelve miles to the village where his aunt lived. I didn't have a gun and I knew there were bears out at night now because of the fish in the creeks but I didn't care. Right now I was more afraid of him than the bears. I had to hurry and get away. I knew he would come looking for me. I knew God would be with me.

I had to wade through a swift running river. It was deep and the water went up over my hip boots to my waist. The water was so cold. I slipped on a rock and almost fell but regained my balance. I was so scared but I made it across okay. The tide was too high to walk along the beach, and the water was right up to the cliffs. I had to climb to the top of the cliffs through the thick alder bushes to get to the village. I was so cold from being wet. I stayed close to the edge of the cliff so I knew I was going the right direction in the dark. I could hear the ocean waves hitting the cliff. I wish I had a flashlight. I didn't want to get lost in the hills.

After walking about four hours I came to his aunt's house a few miles from the village. She was really nice to me and let me stay there that night. I told her about Len and why I had come. She said he was crazy! I dried off and she gave me some clothes to wear and I slept on a blanket on the floor.

I knew the cannery was still operating because the fishing season wasn't over yet. They would also still be operating for the fall season. The next day I went to the cannery and asked for a job and they hired me. Len came looking for me and found me working in the cannery and dragged me outside to the skiff. I was so scared he was going to kill me and I started screaming and tried to get away from him but I couldn't.

The superintendent came out and started towards us to help me but changed his mind, as he knew how crazy Len could be. They had gotten mad at each other before. Len said he was sorry and would be nice to me and that he loved me. I didn't believe him, he is crazy. I started crying. I tried to get away from him but he was too strong and pushed me in the skiff.

He knew I was scared and mad at him and when we got home he didn't talk to me.

This morning Len went out fall fishing with his brother and they would be gone for two weeks. I am so glad I don't have to be with him for a while.

I had been alone for about 10 days. I was getting lonely for someone to talk to besides my dog. I wish I had a radio. I am glad to have my Bible to read. I really miss Ashley and her children.

Today I was so lonesome I took the skiff the twelve miles to the village. I was going pretty fast because the skiff had a 45 horsepower motor on it. All of a sudden I saw a whale at the bow of the boat. It was floating just a foot or two under the water. I pulled up the motor really fast and slid right over it. I could see the blow hole as I went over him. I looked back and it came up out of the water like a big pillar and splashed back down. I thanked God it didn't come up under the skiff and tip it over as I can't swim. It was so nice to visit with Ashley and her children again. I bought a few groceries and went home before dark. I hated to go home but I knew he would come after me again if I wasn't there when he got back.

September 22

Len and Mark got back from fishing late this afternoon, they are through with the fishing season now. They said they did good fishing and caught a lot of fish.

Just before dark a flock of about fifty Canadian geese landed on the sand spit across from our cabin. They wanted me to go with them and I took our dog. The dog got so excited I had to hold onto him so he wouldn't run after them. They shot a couple of geese for us to eat and Mark stayed with us for dinner. They were really good.

We see wolverine and bear tracks by our house on the beach every day. We will have to keep our dog by us when we are outside. Len has been nice to me but I still don't trust him. I have to find a way to leave him, I really hate him and it's not good to hate.

We went in our skiff to a village about twelve miles north of us. Len wanted to play poker with some of the natives there. He had met them while fishing. When you got close to the village you could really smell the fish hanging up outside drying. It smelled really bad. It was a poorer village than ours and everyone lived in tar paper shacks. When we got to theirs it was very small, just two small rooms. About six men and their wives were there, it was very crowded. They played cards late into the night until the next day. The women visited and cooked for everyone. They gave us some bear meat to eat. I had heard bear meat isn't very good unless the cook really knows how to season it. She cooked it so that it tasted really good.

That night I asked the women where the outhouse was. They didn't have one and they said they went in the coffee can on the porch. There were too many people going in and out of the porch and there were no locks on the doors. I went behind some bushes outside even though I was aware of bears that could be around. We went back home when it got light in the morning.

December

This winter was really cold. A storm came in fast this evening with strong winds. We had our skiff anchored out in the water and we went out in the dark with a flashlight to check on it. The beach in front of our house wasn't as protected as our other house was in the bay. We got direct waves from the ocean. Big ice cakes had drifted around the skiff, and big waves were starting to sink it. We had to save the outboard motor from getting wet and sinking so we waded out to take it off the skiff. The water went over our hip boots and was ice cold. We got the motor off the skiff but it was difficult and took awhile to do. We went in the house and put our feet in cold water as our feet had turned blue from frostbite. They hurt but got better after we put them in the cold water. We can't leave our skiff anchored out in the bay overnight anymore. We will have to pull it up above the tide line.

Len's cousin who bought our shack in the village went to Kodiak for the winter. Len asked him if we could stay in our old shack for the winter, and he said we could. I was glad, as I wasn't so scared of him with people close by.

Len wanted to go to his relative's house three and four times a week to play cards. They lived in the village across the bay from us. It was his relative that had thirteen children. Susie, the oldest daughter, who was 18, got married last summer to a man from California. Susie and her husband left the village and moved to San Diego, California. He wanted to live close to his family who lived there. She came back about two months later.

She said he was into wife swapping and so she left him. She divorced him and came back to the village. She said it was really nice in San Diego. It was sunny and hot and people there were swimming in the ocean in December. That was hard to believe, but sounded wonderful. She was pregnant and had her baby at home. She had a really tiny build and I felt sorry for her when she had the baby, she was really screaming. There was no doctor in the village or anything to give her for pain. The baby was premature and blue so they wrapped it in a blanket and put it in the oven to keep it warm. She and the baby survived which we were all very thankful for.

Once she had a bad toothache and kept jabbing the tooth with a needle. It must have done something to the nerve because it stopped aching. We have no dentist here but one man would use pliers to pull out a tooth if someone had a toothache. He had gone for the winter.

December 10

Today I was getting the mail at the village and stopped in to say hi to Nancy, Susie's sister. When I went in the house Nancy had Susie on the floor and was sitting on top of her with a butcher knife. She was going to stab her but I yelled at her to stop. She said she had caught her sister sleeping with her boyfriend, who she was in love with and wanted to marry. Susie ran out of the house and I stayed for a while and talked to Nancy before I went to the store. She was really hurt and I felt sorry for her.

Len insisted on us going to Susie's family every night now to play cards. Len and Susie really started flirting a lot while we all played pinochle.

Tonight she was high on drugs and got really mad at her small baby that was crying and started hitting him hard. Her dad jumped up from his chair and stopped her. He was really mad and yelling at her. I felt so sorry for the baby, she has a really bad temper.

After dinner they all played cards and started drinking a lot. The mother would tell me that she wished she could quit drinking. She liked me to read Bible stories to her as she couldn't read. She was always so nice to me. I went upstairs with the children sometimes and read Bible stories to them that they liked to hear.

Sometimes the men and women would play cards all night and I would put two wooden boxes together to sleep on in the living room.

1975
January

We went to the store today and while I was shopping Len was talking to some men on the dock. He got in a fight with the man he had hit in the face when we were playing bingo a few years ago. Sam socked Len in the face and gave him a bloody nose and a bump on his forehead. He was taken to Susie's mom's house. Someone came and got me from the store. He will have a black eye but is okay. He wouldn't say why they were fighting.

Len wasn't mad or anything but this evening he said he wanted me to go stay with my family and he would charge the airfare and pay for it next fishing season. He said he wanted Susie and her son to come and live with him. I was thinking this was why he sent me out in the storm hoping I would die so he could be with her. All he had to do was tell me. I would have been so happy to leave him. She was a couple of years younger than me but not very nice, or good looking. She has a bad temper but if he loves her I am happy for them. I said okay, I was so glad. I really didn't love him anymore.

I caught a plane and flew to Seattle. It was so good to see my family again. I stayed with one of my sisters today. I got to visit my parents and all six of my brothers and sisters. I had such a good time with my family. Today I have been here two weeks.

I was at my parent's house one day and there was a knock at the door and my dad said it was Len. I was so scared. He told my dad he wanted to talk to me. He was really sorry and said he loved me and would never drink again and would be faithful to me. He pleaded with me to go back with him to the village, and he started crying.

My parents saw him crying and felt sorry for him. I can't

believe they feel sorry for him. They said they thought I should go with him, and give him another chance. I couldn't believe they were saying that. I didn't have a chance to be alone long enough with them to tell them everything about my marriage. They just didn't understand and they didn't have any place for me to stay and money to help me. I wish I knew where to go to get help and a place to stay until I could get work.

I didn't feel sorry for him and I didn't believe him! I was so scared of him I felt sick and really hated to go back with him, but I did. We caught a plane that day and went back to the village. When we got to Anchorage he bought a case of whiskey. I told him that he had promised not to drink anymore. He said he was buying it for his uncle. I thought to myself I bet it's not for his uncle. When we got to the village he wanted to take the case of whiskey to Susie's for his uncle.

When we got there she came up to me and asked me to go upstairs with her. When we got up there she told me she stayed with Len and slept with him. I told her that I already knew that. I said I didn't care, I didn't love him anymore. I had just come back because he was crying and wanted me to and I didn't have any place to stay in Washington.

Len started drinking with the men downstairs. And after they had been drinking for a while Susie's mother came running upstairs where I was visiting with the children. She said the men were going to shoot each other and she wanted me to come and stop them. I said no, I was not going to do that. Let them shoot each other.

Somehow she calmed them down and after a while I went downstairs and Len and I walked home. He was drunk.

On the way home he wanted to stop at his uncle Pete's. They were drinking whiskey and he started drinking with them and taking drugs. He took a bottle of whiskey and grabbed me, and tried to force me to drink. I was able to get away from him because he was so drunk, and I ran home. That really scared me. I never wanted to become addicted to alcohol or drugs after seeing how it destroyed marriages and people's lives. He came home a little later and passed out on the bed.

I planned to leave him for good. There must be some relative of mine that would take me in until I can find work. This time I knew I would never come back to him. I packed my Bible, some pictures, and my mother's letters in a small overnight bag and hid it under the bed. The next morning I knew the mail plane was coming in about eight o'clock and I was going to ask the pilot to let me charge the airfare. I knew Len would be sleeping late because of the drinking he had done the night before.

It had been snowing a lot and the snow was really deep up to the top of my hip boots. I had to walk through the snow on the bank above the beach. The tide was high so I couldn't walk on the sandy beach to get to the village. I just got to the village as the plane landed. The pilot said he would take me to King Salmon, so I could get a plane to Anchorage. He knew how Len had treated me.

Some of the people in the village came to meet the plane and saw me and gave me money. Susie said she was sorry about what she did with Len and gave me the money she had in her pocket. Her younger sister Nancy gave me money and her shoes so I wouldn't have to wear my hip boots on the plane and in the Seattle airport. The shoes were big on me and it was hard to keep them on but I was thankful for them. I gave her my boots. Everyone was so nice to me. I boarded the plane and kept reading my Bible and praying to God to help me escape.

We landed in King Salmon and the office at the airport had gotten a message on the shortwave radio. It was from Len, and he said he was coming after me to kill me. He said if he couldn't have me no one else would either. He had left our village on a small plane and was on his way to King Salmon. The pilot had been told on his radio about Len. He was told to fly him around and not land until the jet I was on took off. Len caught on after a while to what the pilot was doing and told him he would kill him if he didn't land so he landed the plane. I was in the jet and the doors were closed but Len ran onto the runway and stood in front of the plane.

As four men pulled him off the runway, he saw me through the window and was glaring at me as we took off.

I knew one of the couples on the plane, they were always so

nice to me. The woman's husband got up from his seat and told me if I ever wanted a job fishing he would hire me to run his snag skiff. I thought that was so nice of him, but I would never come back here again.

The airport in King Salmon sent a message to the Anchorage airport about Len trying to follow me by plane and kill me. When I got there the stewardess told me which airline counter to go to. Len's relative's had bought tickets for me and the airline had held the plane for me. It was like a miracle, they were so nice to do that for me. They had two men in the baggage department find my little overnight bag for me. I thanked God for always being there for me.

I arrived in Seattle at 4:00 am and didn't want to wake up my mother and father that early so I stayed in the airport until 9:00 before I called them. They were so surprised and glad to see me. I told them I left Len and wanted to get a divorce, and told them what happened. They agreed with me and said they would help me. Len knew where my parents lived so I stayed with my sister. They were trying to hide me from him.

January 24

My parents came this evening to see me and Len must have followed them. My sister went to close the drapes by the sofa and he was standing by the window looking in. She screamed and shut the drapes. I was so scared. The door wasn't locked and he came inside. He grabbed my arm and started dragging me to the door. I was screaming and trying to get away but he was too strong.

My dad went to the phone right away and called the police. He yelled at Len that he had called the police and to let me go. Dad started towards him and he let me go and took off running. He got in the car and was leaving when the police came. I heard the police on the loud speaker telling him to pull over but he didn't so they cornered him. He wouldn't get out of the car so they broke the window and got him out. They said he was drunk and on drugs. They put him in jail for a couple of days.

I applied for a divorce and everything was ready in two days. I didn't try to get any of what little assets we had. I just wanted to get away from him. They had to let him out of jail. He told the police he was going to go to the courthouse and kill everyone. They had police outside the door in case he showed up but he never did.

My aunt sent me enough money to buy an airline ticket to her house in another state. I stayed with her until I got a job and could get my own place. I changed my name, because I heard from my family that after fishing season he hired a detective and gave him $20,000 to find me. My family said he harassed them all every day trying to get them to tell him where I was. My dad talked him into going to a counselor at church. The counselor said Len threatened to kill him because he wouldn't tell him where I was. He said Len was crazy. He also threatened to kill the minister at church.

After the shooting incident Len had always been so hateful and mad at everyone in the village and towards the superintendant of the Alaska Packers Cannery. He told me about two months before I left him how he had a plan to burn the cannery down by using gas in a can. I never really thought he would. He was always talking about how he was going to kill the two young men that shot at him and shot me.

Right after I left him I heard the cannery burned down. Nancy later married the man she loved and sent my mother a picture to give to me of her and the baby. She said she would understand if I didn't write to her because of Len. She wanted me to see the picture of her and the baby. I thought that was so nice of her. I wish I could have written to her and thanked her. Everyone in the village had been so nice to me.

Len died in Anchorage January 20, 2010.